KELLY HOPPEN'S
Essential **Style Solutions** for **Every Home**

To my grandson Rudy, with love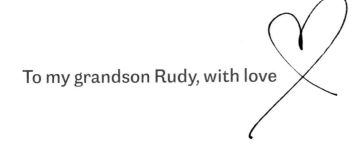

FRANCES LINCOLN

KELLY
HOPPEN'S

Essential Style Solutions
for Every Home

Love
Kelly Hoppen

More so than ever before, our home is our sanctuary. We live in a world that is constantly changing and very different from what we have been used to during the past few years, but we all still want and need to be surrounded by beauty, warmth, luxury and practicality.

Having designed interiors for more than 40 years, I am as passionate about it today as I was when I first started. I live and breathe design, and am constantly thinking about the way we live and how we interact in different spaces. With my knowledge and years of experience, I have learned that it isn't just about the way things look – how we feel, the experiences we have, the understanding of what we need and what we crave, and how we share all this with whom we live is just as important. The beauty of design is that you really do have a blank canvas, even if your vision is not always possible to realize immediately.

With more and more people needing to create multifaceted spaces under one roof, I hope this book will encourage you to question yourself and your needs, as much as it will inspire you to push all the boundaries to create the timeless interiors you desire.

I have created this small-format book so it's easy to carry around and use when you're choosing designs for your home, wherever you are.

Always take time to create these spaces, and shoot for the stars with whatever you desire. Then budget and plan as much as you can before you begin. I am so excited to share my passion, knowledge and secret tools with you.

Most of all, have fun!

Love always,

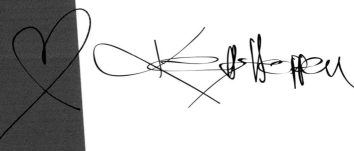

CONTENTS

1

Introduction

Everyone has the ability to create a home that's right for them. The first step is to ask: what does home mean to you?

I've been designing homes,
as well as other spaces, for
more than 40 years now.
Early on in my career I was
given some great advice by a life
coach: the one thing that helps
you learn and grow in business is
to share your knowledge. I've never
forgotten that, and it's why I wanted
to write this book. I truly believe
that anyone can create a home that
is both beautiful and practical,
whatever size budget and space
they're working with. There's no real
mystery to it, but you do need to do the
groundwork and plan carefully to avoid
making expensive mistakes. Over the
following pages I'll share my top tips and my
tried-and-tested design techniques to help
you make your ideas come to life and create
the home you've only dared to dream about.

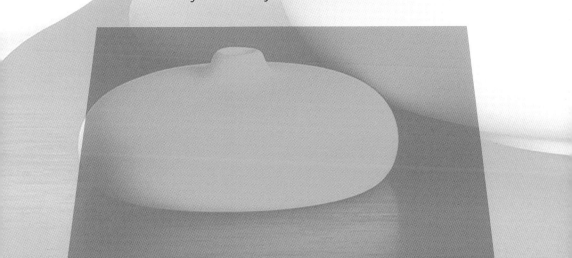

COMING HOME

Home should be your ultimate haven, a space that feels inviting and welcoming, comfortable and secure. Wherever you live – in the city or country, in an apartment or house – when you open the front door and step inside, you will want to feel like you have left all your worries behind and can breathe again.

WELCOME HOME!

I don't think anyone would argue with that. So how do you capture that wonderful feeling and create a space where you can close the door on anything that's making you feel stressed, and just relax and be yourself?

HOW DO YOU WANT YOUR HOME TO FEEL?

A home is a highly personal space and what works for one person or family won't necessarily suit another. When I work on home designs with clients, one of the first things I ask them is how they want their home to *feel*. It's so important that a home works for whoever lives in it on an emotional level as well as a practical one, and this is something that often gets overlooked. For it to truly feel like 'home' – whatever that means for you – the ambience and style of a space must feel right. This means that every choice you make – from the colour of your walls and the materials you choose for your floors to the style of your furniture and even the way your home smells – should make you feel uplifted and energized, relaxed and peaceful, comfortable and safe.

Another aspect to consider is the impression your home makes on others, especially if you're someone who likes to entertain. In this case, you might prioritize creating that wow factor, to blow the minds of your guest when they step inside.

This collection of panama hats makes a simple but unusual display on an otherwise plain white wall. This was in a beach house in Barbados and the hats were all sourced locally. It's a great idea for an entrance hall, as it's both practical and full of impact.

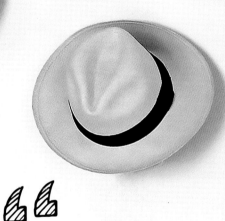

BE TRUE TO YOURSELF

Once you have considered the impression you want your home to make – on yourself and those you live with, and on others who come to your home as guests – you can start to build up your scheme from there. The key principle to remember is that your home is your personal space and should reflect your lifestyle and personality. Your needs and priorities will depend on whether you live alone, with a partner or a friend, or a large family or a pet – but try to be realistic about this so you design a home that works for you and how you live now.

Think about what you love and what makes you uniquely *you* – do this exercise as an individual, a couple or a family. Take inspiration from your travels and your passions. What colours make your heart sing? What textures can you not resist running your fingers over? Do you find minimal spaces appealing or love the intrigue of collections that tell a story? Are you drawn to light, white, open-plan and breezy spaces or do you like cosy rooms that are moody and dramatic?

A home should be individual to whoever lives there, so personal displays that reflect character are everything.

Once you have jotted down some key words that sum up the general mood and feel you want to create for your home, you need to look at each space in detail and think very hard about what you want from it and how best to achieve it. If knocking down walls and changing the layout isn't an option, you need to be realistic about what you can do with the space that you have. Really get acquainted with each space in turn and make a note of its good and bad points. Some things to consider are:

- **How much natural light does it get and how does that change during the day?**

- **Are there any architectural features that you'd like to restore, transform, highlight or disguise?**

- **What are the dimensions?**

- **How does it connect with other areas?**

BE YOUR OWN INTERIOR DESIGNER

When I design for clients, not only do I need to get to know the space I'm going to be working with, but I also have to get into their heads. I need to discover their likes and dislikes, their needs, wants and priorities, their hopes and dreams – and what their lifestyle is like. Only then can I create a home that both looks great and works for them on every level. There's no point in designing a state-of-the-art kitchen for someone who dislikes cooking, or a wonderful bathroom with a bathtub as the star piece when everyone prefers showers. Ask yourself the following questions:

- **What will the room be used for? List all the activities that will need to take place here. Most rooms in modern homes need to be multifunctional to some degree.**

- **What time – or times – of day will you mostly be using the space?**

- **How much natural light does the room get and what do the windows look out on?**

- **What are the key pieces of furniture you will need here?**

- **How much storage will you need in this room and what type?**

Whatever style and tone you choose for your home should be evident right from the entrance, as it's the first space people see.

A statement staircase is one of my favourite ways to make an impact. This flowing design of dark wood and glass leads the eye up, while the unexpectedly low-hanging Terzani chain-mail pendant light adds further texture and interest.

ALWAYS MAKE A GOOD FIRST IMPRESSION

SMART PLANNING

Every project is different – in scale, style and financial outlay – but there are a few strategies you can employ to help you ensure things run as smoothly as possible and give you the results you want. Absolutely essential is having a clear, firm vision of what you want to achieve, within a realistic timeframe and budget; then, careful planning is everything.

There are so many possibilities for different styles, materials and suppliers – for everything from fixtures, fittings and furniture to paint, flooring and fabrics – that the choices can feel overwhelming and make it impossible to make decisions and stick to them.

My first tip is to get a large notebook in which you can jot down ideas, make lists of what you need to do when, and keep a note of key measurements, paint colours and suppliers. As you gather samples of fabrics and other materials, label each one with the supplier, name or reference number and possible use. As your thoughts start to come together, write yourself a design brief, as you would for a third-party interior designer. This will help you to crystallize your ideas and keep focused on the end goal.

I'm a very visual person and I tend to work instinctively. I can tell very quickly what combinations of textures, colours, tones and shapes will give me the look I want. To explain how to pull a room scheme together, I often use the wardrobe analogy: you dress for the occasion – a country walk, an important meeting, a dinner date; you start with a key piece – jeans, a sharp jacket, a knockout dress – and you build your look up from there; then you accessorize. What you never do is wear all the clothes you like at once.

An eclectic mix of furniture, vintage and new, defines this living space, with the layout echoing the architectural grid of the gallery balcony and tall steel-framed Crittall windows. Tones, textures and form are all in perfect balance.

Kelly's Planning Checklist

GETTING STARTED

- [ ] Get to know your home and yourself.
- [ ] Assess the natural light levels and think about how you can work with them.
- [ ] Draw up a realistic budget, including a 20% contingency, and plan the project accordingly.
- [ ] Identify your priorities — you may not be able to do everything on your wish list.

THE PRACTICALITIES

- [ ] Write a brief and start gathering samples.
- [ ] Draw floor plans to scale, so you can decide on the best layout for furniture and lighting.
- [ ] Discuss key delivery dates with your contractors to guard against hold-ups.
- [ ] Write a schedule of work and monitor it.

Function and space lie at the heart of good design. These are key aspects to consider and will help you to determine every other design decision you make, from where the sofa is placed to the decorating palette. The chances are, some rooms will need to serve more than one purpose – a spare room that doubles as a gym or yoga studio; a dining area that by day is a home office; a living room that is used for relaxing, watching TV and entertaining.

ZONE & FLOW

As well as being multipurpose, spaces in many modern homes are often open-plan. Walls have been knocked down between rooms, and narrow hallways have been opened up to increase the sense of volume and create light, airy interiors. The challenge is to design these spaces so that different zones are defined, separate areas are created, and the spaces flow seamlessly together.

I have always found it easy to visualize a space in 3-D – my brain just works that way – but I know that many people find it difficult. The trick is to think of a room as six planes – floor, ceiling and four walls, not forgetting windows and doors, which can provide delightful opportunities for decorative details and embellishments. The materials, colours and tones on each of these surfaces need to work together and complement each other, with a rich mix of textures to surprise the eye and invite touch. With regards to flow, think about how you move between areas and around furniture, as well as the vistas from different angles.

This desk is positioned for the best view, through the living area and beyond, while dark oak slats run up the wall behind it and across the ceiling, leading the eye.

BALANCE & HARMONY

Key to creating a calming, yet energizing and uplifting interior that is a joy to be in, is achieving a sense of balance and harmony. Think of this as the invigorating tension between opposites, the complementary frisson in contrast and the negative space around objects. It is this yin and yang of interior design that gives a home a sense of cordial vitality and interest.

CREATING SYMMETRY DOESN'T MEAN MIRROR IMAGE

Whether you are designing a whole room, hanging pictures on the wall or curating a display of objects for shelves or a tabletop or mantelpiece, creating balance is as much about what you leave out as what you put in – rather like the white space around the characters in calligraphy. This also means you can edit your arrangements from time to time, swapping items in and out of storage to create a seasonal change and keep things looking fresh.

SYMMETRY

An important aspect of balance is symmetry, as it makes a space feel calming, welcoming and easy on the eye, where nothing jars or feels out of place. The trick, however, is not to make one side of a room the exact mirror image of the other but instead sympathetic to it, with echoing aspects – such as a repeated shape, material or texture, or an accent colour picked up and used in a different way. Always ensure there is something slightly 'off', to surprise the eye and prevent the effect from seeming sterile and flat.

This vast living area epitomizes balance, with the seating areas arranged symmetrically around the central column. Understated differences enliven the echoing elements, while textural and tonal contrasts bring vitality to the off-white and wood scheme.

OPPOSITES ATTRACT

Creating playful contrasts is a great way to achieve a feeling of balance in a room. This is where the dualistic philosophy of yin and yang comes into play. Think about the complementary and interconnected relationships between the following pairs:

- Light and dark
- Rough and smooth
- Matt and shiny
- Opaque and transparent
- Hard and soft
- Straight and curved
- Antique and modern

All of these complementary but contrasting pairs work well in juxtaposition because one offsets the other and enhances its quality. This is also a great way to enliven a neutral colour palette, as mixing up textures and tones instantly creates interest without making the overall result too busy. One of my favourite techniques is to contrast fabrics, especially with natural linen, which is so versatile. Consider the stunning combinations of fine sheer curtains alongside a coarse linen blind; a wide silk band around a linen cushion; or a rich velvet cushion against linen upholstery – so simple but so effective.

PROPORTION, SCALE & FORM

The simplicity of repetition and alignment has always appealed to me, as it offers a straightforward way to achieve that sense of calm tranquillity that I want from a space. But I always like to break things up with something unpredictable, to add drama and impact.

Eastern interior style has always inspired me and the classic 'East meets West' look has become one of my style signatures. The ideas of simplicity and balance originated in the East and are the foundation of my work. Emphasizing the symmetry in a room – or creating it where necessary – is the easiest way to make a space feel balanced. In a room with imperfect proportions, a sense of symmetry can be achieved through the clever use of materials and the choice and placement of furniture.

Using runners is one of my signature techniques for improving the proportions of a room, increasing a sense of volume, drawing the eye or connecting spaces together. They can be vertical or horizontal, along walls, floors or ceilings; I even use them on furniture and soft furnishings. They might be in a different, toning or contrasting colour, but are always a change of texture or material.

The clever use of fabric elevates this dining area from simple to chic. Linen panels on the wall form a neutral backdrop, while long gold runners under each place setting add drama.

BALANCE, HARMONY, CONTRAST, CALM, YIN & YANG

EAST MEETS WEST IS ONE OF MY SIGNATURE LOOKS

PERFECTLY BALANCED, EASY STYLE

THE JOY OF RUNNERS

Runners provide the perfect opportunity to bring contrasting materials and textures together in order to highlight and offset the qualities of each. Think of the grain and patina of a dark-stained wood floor inset with a shiny metal runner, the random patterning on a marble panel running through a plain plaster wall, or natural linen panels hung to create instant warmth and simple texture.

As well as being a useful way to alter the proportions of a space, define different zones within it and emphasize the design grid (see page 22), runners also offer the chance to introduce a small quantity of an expensive material or finish that in larger expanses would blow the budget. This is the way to ensure your design scheme includes that hand-printed wallpaper, expensive stone, artisan tile or de luxe fabric you've set your heart on.

PERFECT PLACEMENT

The furniture and objects you choose and how you arrange them is a key part of creating a balanced interior. If space allows, pairs of items such as sofas, armchairs, ottomans, side tables and lamps are an obvious way to impose symmetry.

I also love to juxtapose furniture and objects in unexpected ways, such as offsetting hard, straight lines with organic shapes and rounded edges. Even a simple curved dish set on a square table, or round or irregularly shaped objects arranged along linear shelves or displayed within architectural niches, can be surprisingly effective. Another great trick is to introduce an oversized item – a piece of furniture, a sculptural light or an up-scaled headboard, perhaps. This creates a focal point and injects instant vitality into a space.

Creative lighting enhances a display: here, a combination of warm-white LED strips and 12v halogen spotlights.

Set into a niche in a master bedroom, its opulent gold surface highlighted by concealed lighting, this luxe de Gournay wallpaper makes a glamorous statement, perfectly balanced by the simple display of identical vases on the dark wood shelf.

THE DESIGN GRID

I see every space I design as a blank canvas, a cube with six planes on which I start to construct a grid of vertical and horizontal lines. This structure can be used to alter proportions, link the planes of a room, form connections between areas, align furniture and frame views.

LOOK AT YOUR SPACE IN A DIFFERENT WAY

EMPHASIZE THE VERTICAL AND HORIZONTAL LINES IN A SPACE

" The grid forms the bone structure of a space. It's the foundation upon which the rest of the design is built. "

Every element in this space reinforces the grid, from the internal joinery that frames different areas and the stone runner leading through the corridor to the curtain rail and the leather trim on the rug.

ECHO THE GRID WITH EVERY ELEMENT

STRUCTURAL ELEMENTS ARE KEY COMPONENTS OF THE GRID

HOPPEN AT HOME

When I bought my London home (opposite), a former auction house, it was an empty shell, with a towering ceiling supported on a series of structural columns. I took advantage of these columns to help me divide up the ground-floor space into different zones, using them as the starting point for my grid and making a feature of them in the finished design. In keeping with the tonal scheme, I clad them with pale wood panels, inset with slim horizontal nickel and bronze runners for a touch of glamour. These frame different areas beautifully and are echoed by the floor-to-ceiling slatted wood doors – my modern interpretation of traditional Japanese shoji screens – and the taupe linen curtains, which both accentuate the height of the room. The horizontals, meanwhile, are defined by the long, low marble shelf that I use for display and the lines and placement of the furniture and art.

While the vertical and horizontal lines of the grid are emphasized by the wood panels, marble shelf and sofa, focus is brought to the mid-point of the space by the position of the art and the pendant lights.

The subtle pattern and tonal variations of the matt parquet floor add understated interest.

USING A GRID

When designing a space, it's important that you work in three dimensions and consider every cross-section – not just the walls, floor and ceiling but the mid-points, too. You can draw the focus with furniture or lamps, or by hanging art, shelves or pendant lights.

Incorporating structural or architectural features – including doors, windows and fireplaces – is always a great starting point for planning the design grid and furniture layout. Remember that emphasizing the horizontals – such as with floating shelves, skirting boards and picture rails– can make a space seem longer or wider, while defining the verticals – for instance, with runners or panels, tall furniture, doors or floor-to-ceiling curtains – will make the ceiling seem higher.

MIXING MATERIALS

An effective way to define the grid is to mix materials by introducing runners. These could take the form of slim strips or wider panels, and run through floors, up walls or stairs, and across ceilings. Whether you make a bold statement with contrasting colours or a subtle shift of textures in a tonal scheme is up to you.

CREATING FOCAL POINTS

Every design should include something surprising to catch the eye and create a sense of theatre. This could be a single show-stopping piece of furniture, lighting or art, a personal display, or a sumptuous material or finish – but whatever it is, it must have a wow factor.

STATEMENT PIECES ADD DRAMA AND INTEREST

The focus is drawn to the Gold Senza Titolo artwork by Gavin Turk and the Rabbit Construction sculpture by Gimhongsok, set on a backlit plinth at the end of a runner in the parquet floor.

Introducing an element of drama and intrigue to a space by incorporating a star piece or finish, or adding a touch of something unexpected, helps to lift a scheme and give it personality and vitality. As well as delivering the all-important wow factor, cleverly positioned focal points also contribute to the flow of the space. Because they attract attention, these points of interest can be used to punctuate a space, to draw the eye along a corridor, for example, or through a doorway, positioned so that the door surround frames them in an imposing way, creating a theatrical vista.

When it comes to star pieces, less is more. These show-stoppers are show-offs and need space to breathe, so make sure you don't detract from the effect by adding too much else around them. Think about the backdrop and lighting, too, and ensure they set off your piece to best effect.

DRAMATIC, ARRESTING, INTRIGUING CENTREPIECE

The epitome of bold glamour: my Paul Vanstone sculpture is displayed to striking effect on a plinth covered in gold de Gournay wallpaper in front of a dramatic runner of shiny black specialist plasterwork.

POSITION YOUR STAR PIECE TO CREATE MAXIMUM IMPACT

SHELF ART

The creative possibilities offered by shelves are endless. As well as serving a practical purpose by meeting storage needs, shelves provide a blank canvas for displaying much-loved objects or collections, books, pictures, plants, flowers or candles.

Personal items, photographs and treasured objects bring a home to life.

I love the simplicity of displaying multiple identical objects in an irregular way.

The sliding frames on this shelving unit I designed can be moved along to square off and highlight different areas of the display.

The style of shelves you choose is an important design decision that needs to be considered at the offset, as an integral part of your overall room scheme. Single floating shelves, built-in shelving units or free-standing dressers can all be used to emphasize the grid and make a style statement.

● First assess what you want to display and where – consider size, shape, colour, quantity and configuration.

● Are you planning to source a free-standing shelving unit or dresser, or have something custom-built?

● Do you need a tall multi-shelf unit or a single low-level floating shelf?

● How will this work within your grid? Do you want to accentuate the height or width of your space?

● What style and materials are you drawn to? Something with presence – solid and chunky, dark wood or marble; something unobtrusive that blends into the background – pale wood, lacquered, Perspex or painted to match the walls; or something vintage with a timeworn character and patina?

Once these decisions have been made you can go to town arranging your displays. This is your chance to showcase your treasures and let your personality shine through.

The curves of the sculptural Albedo ●—➤ lamp by Lahumière Design offset the straight lines of the dark wood shelf and propped-up picture frames — an easy way to add height to a display.

A UNIFIED COLLECTION WILL ALWAYS BE EASY ON THE EYE

Sometimes simplicity is best. This collection of delicate matt white porcelain stands out beautifully against the soft sheen and grain of the solid black oak shelf. The result is a perfectly balanced, restful arrangement.

MOVE THINGS AROUND UNTIL YOU GET THE LOOK YOU WANT

CREATE BALANCE BY PLACING TALLER ITEMS TOWARDS THE BACK

A PERSONAL EDIT

Choosing what pieces to have on display in a home is highly personal and reveals a lot about the identity and lifestyle of those who live in it. One person may have a passion for simple white porcelain, mid-century ceramics or coloured glassware; another may be a collector of rare books, vinyl records or contemporary sculpture. Others may have an eclectic mix of possessions accumulated on travels abroad, or just on the journey of life – treasured objects, photographs and family heirlooms that spark a lifetime of memories of places and people. All these belongings tell a story about who you are. They bring a home to life and give it character and atmosphere; above all, they make it feel like home.

Deciding where and how to showcase these items is key. The aim is to create a display that complements the overall setting and style of the room, one that adds interest and draws the eye but doesn't jar. Take into account both the design grid and the furniture layout, and make sure your display will look good from the main seating areas and as you move into and through the space. Consider, too, the colours and textures of what you are displaying as well as those used in the room as a whole, and make sure there is one or more common theme to pull everything together.

When you are composing the arrangement itself, as with a room as a whole, think balance not symmetry. First select your main centrepiece and build outwards from there, juxtaposing different shapes, heights, textures and colours, but ensuring there's a unifying theme. Play around with the composition until you are happy with it; then revisit it after a break and reassess. Sometimes, taking one or two things out can make all the difference – a bit of breathing space around belongings often gives them space to sing. I also like to refresh my displays by changing things around from time to time.

REPETITION & ORDER

Even the most mundane collection of everyday objects can be elevated into a stunning work of art if it is displayed well. The impact of an orderly row of identical simple objects should never be underestimated. A fail-safe way to impose order is to arrange items to reflect the grid, or in rows or groups of two or more. If in doubt, three is usually the magic number.

The colours, shapes and textures of the eclectic pieces on display stand out strikingly against the backdrop of matt black wood. Leaving clear space around objects lets them breathe and gives a more balanced effect.

TREASURED
POSSESSIONS
TELL THE STORIES
OF YOUR LIFE

2

First Principles of Style

There are certain aspects of designing a home that should never be overlooked — here are those key considerations.

However ambitious or modest your project, you can't go far wrong if you give due thought to the essential elements that ultimately work together to create a successful interior, one that is welcoming, comfortable, practical and stylish. These are tone and colour – a palette of hues that harmonize and complement each other; texture – a rich mix of materials and finishes that play off one another; light – for both function and ambience; and finishing touches – the interiors equivalent to accessorizing an outfit, the details that add a wow factor and elevate the mood. All these elements should be considered in their own right and in relation to one another, as they are the different layers that are put together to create something amazing.

TONES & COLOURS

When it comes to interior colour schemes, people typically associate my work with a neutral palette. Chic, soothing and endlessly versatile, neutrals are anything but boring and I love using them because they provide the perfect, quiet, easy backdrop for so many looks, materials and styles of furniture and furnishings – not to mention accent colours.

Pops of bold colour lift a monochrome scheme, and red and black is a classic mix.

From chic, smart black and white, through all the shades of grey, taupe and sand, to creams and off-whites, neutrals work – regardless of whether your interior style is minimalist or decorative, or you're drawn to the clean lines of contemporary furniture or the history and patina of antique or vintage pieces. They also look beautiful with all kinds of natural materials – pale or dark wood, stone and marble.

CHOOSING A COLOUR SCHEME

A good starting point is to look in your wardrobe – the colours and tones you dress in are probably those that make you feel good. Trust your instinct and start with the shades you're naturally drawn to and build up your colour palette from there. Try to decide on the larger expanses of the room first, as they will obviously have the most impact. They key thing is to stick with colours that work well tonally – warm hues sit together comfortably, while cooler shades also complement each other, but mixing the two will throw your scheme off kilter. Think about textures, too (see page 66), as colours look different depending on whether they reflect or absorb light. The most important thing is to assess colours in the space they're intended for, at different times of the day.

A NEUTRAL
SCHEME PROMOTES
A SENSE OF CALM

In this off-white space, the ribbed upholstery,
wool carpet and curtain, with its geometric
cut-out design, add layers of interest and
ensure the effect isn't flat.

PALE & FRESH

Light, bright, crisp and clean, white interiors are both versatile and timeless. They suit all styles of furniture, furnishings and materials, and can be contrasted with black or other strong colours, such as green, red or navy, or blended with subtler shades of grey, taupe or sand.

TEXTURAL CONTRAST IS EVERYTHING

The strong lines of the Baltus frame chair, upholstered in off-white linen, are softened by the addition of a taupe linen cushion with a wide band of pale velvet.

For understated glamour, you can't beat the simplicity of a tone-on-tone decorating scheme in shades of fresh white. Think of an all-white interior with cool stone, marble or resin floors and furnishings in crisp cottons and pale linens, with billowy sheer curtains at the shuttered windows. This style of room is almost synonymous with hot, sunny climates, but whites work well in colder regions, too. It all comes down to texture – picture milk-white faux fur or sheepskin rugs in front of a fireplace, cashmere blankets on brushed cotton upholstery, deep velvet borders on natural linen drapes at the windows, and touches of buttery leather and suede on cushion bands and trims. Layering up a rich mix of textures is the key to any successful room scheme, but especially tone-on-tone or monochrome spaces, which could otherwise seem flat and unwelcoming.

I always start planning a room scheme with a pile of different fabrics, at least one of which will always be linen – a great, versatile base fabric for almost any interior. I invariably won't use all of these fabrics, but somehow the feel I want for the space evolves through this process. I then start to build up a mood board, including all the other elements.

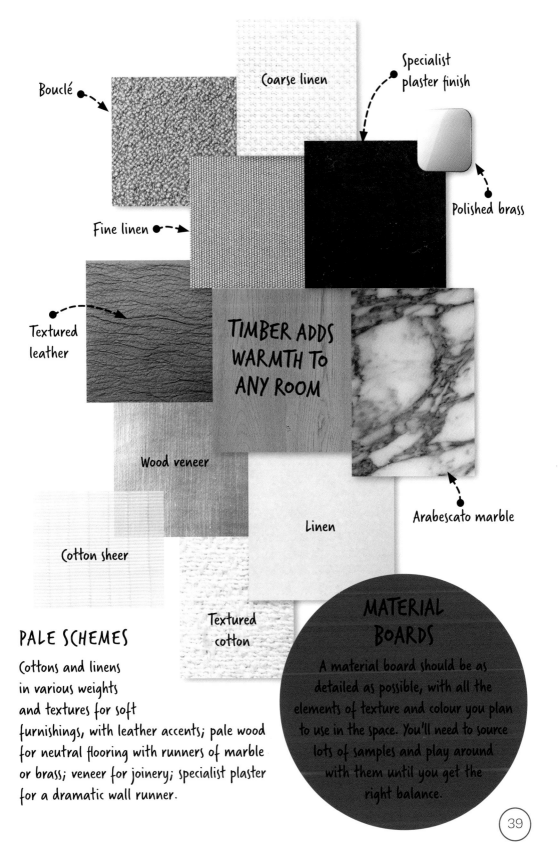

Bouclé

Coarse linen

Specialist plaster finish

Polished brass

Fine linen

Textured leather

TIMBER ADDS WARMTH TO ANY ROOM

Wood veneer

Arabescato marble

Cotton sheer

Linen

Textured cotton

PALE SCHEMES

Cottons and linens in various weights and textures for soft furnishings, with leather accents; pale wood for neutral flooring with runners of marble or brass; veneer for joinery; specialist plaster for a dramatic wall runner.

MATERIAL BOARDS

A material board should be as detailed as possible, with all the elements of texture and colour you plan to use in the space. You'll need to source lots of samples and play around with them until you get the right balance.

Black-and-white photography, including Accordionist, Esztergom, October 21, 1916, by André Kertész, stands out against the white wall.

THE PICTURE FRAMES AND FURNITURE LINES DEFINE THE GRID.

BLACK AND WHITE IS ALWAYS A CHIC PAIRING

The clean-lined dark wenge dining table is in dramatic contrast to the white walls and echoes the picture frames.

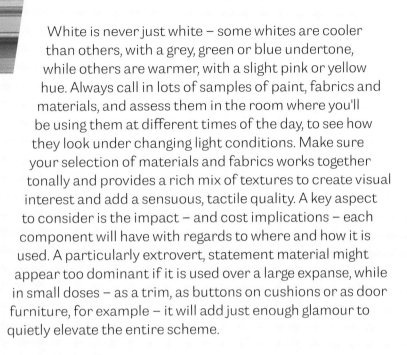

White is never just white – some whites are cooler than others, with a grey, green or blue undertone, while others are warmer, with a slight pink or yellow hue. Always call in lots of samples of paint, fabrics and materials, and assess them in the room where you'll be using them at different times of the day, to see how they look under changing light conditions. Make sure your selection of materials and fabrics works together tonally and provides a rich mix of textures to create visual interest and add a sensuous, tactile quality. A key aspect to consider is the impact – and cost implications – each component will have with regards to where and how it is used. A particularly extrovert, statement material might appear too dominant if it is used over a large expanse, while in small doses – as a trim, as buttons on cushions or as door furniture, for example – it will add just enough glamour to quietly elevate the entire scheme.

TIMELESS STYLE

I love the simplicity of plain white walls paired with dark wood joinery, doors and floors. You can stain original floorboards if they're in good enough condition – a little wear and tear adds character. This combination, for me, is eternally smart, stylish and versatile, as it can be layered and dressed up as you wish – with contemporary furniture or vintage pieces, with pops of colour or other neutral tones, and, of course, layer upon layer of texture. I find that repeating materials and colours in adjacent spaces is the easiest way to create a sense of flow between them.

 Plain white walls create a gallery-like backdrop that is ideal for showcasing art, photographs and displays.

WARM NEUTRALS

The family of neutrals with warmer, slightly yellow or orange undertones bridges the gap between fresh white and deeper taupe. Encompassing all the shades of cream through to pale biscuit, they work especially well with earthy tones and black.

Warm neutrals create comfortable, welcoming interiors and tend to suit either bright sunny rooms or those that are generally lit with the soft golden glow of artificial lighting. They pair beautifully with natural materials, such as rich-coloured wood and soft leather or suede, and stone or marble with warm undertones. The effect is easy on the eye and liveable, yet smart and chic.

As always, textural contrast is key to adding interest and depth to warm neutral interiors. Consider how things feel as well as how they look, and make sure you create a feast for the fingers and feet as well as the eyes. For instance, think of smooth silk, soft wool, sumptuous velvet and coarse linen alongside the natural grain of wood, cool metal and glass or hard stone.

Self-patterned and damask fabrics are a great way to introduce subtle pattern into a scheme, while small doses of statement fabrics – perhaps crushed velvet, pleated silk or lace – can be brought in for textural contrast. Clever details, such as a contrasting trim, band or runner, an unexpected fringe or an oversized button can make all the difference to the overall design and provide just enough interest to elevate furnishings a long way out of the ordinary.

Damask upholstery is contrasted with a paler linen cushion adorned with a large shiny black horn button.

Cushion bands in contrasting textures and either toning or accent colours are one of my signature designs. This taupe linen sofa is enhanced by the off-white linen cushion with its wide velvet band.

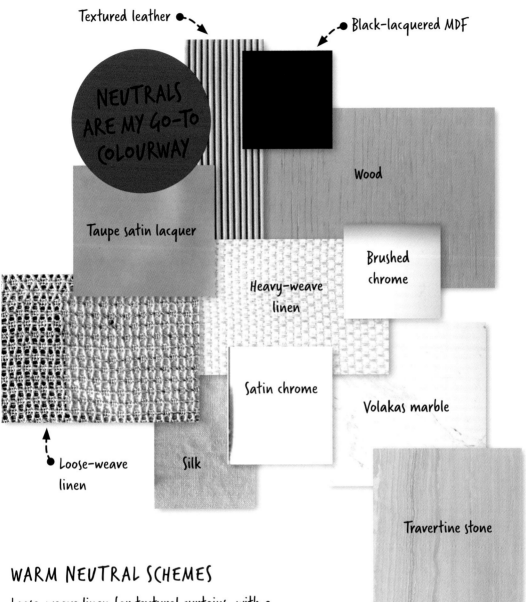

Textured leather

Black-lacquered MDF

NEUTRALS ARE MY GO-TO COLOURWAY

Wood

Taupe satin lacquer

Brushed chrome

Heavy-weave linen

Satin chrome

Volakas marble

Loose-weave linen

Silk

Travertine stone

WARM NEUTRAL SCHEMES

Loose-weave linen for textural curtains, with a silk edging or trim for contrast; heavy-weave linen and leather for upholstery with the other fabrics repeated for cushions. Stone or wood for the flooring with runners of marble; wood for the doors with panels of taupe lacquer and handles or runners of chrome; lacquered MDF for shelves with chrome detailing.

SLEEK ACCENTS KEEP THE SCHEME CONTEMPORARY

Kelly's Top Five

UPHOLSTERY FABRICS
----

01 LINEN
02 VELVET
03 LEATHER/SUEDE
04 BOUCLÉ
05 DAMASK

LINEN IS OFTEN THE HERO
OF A ROOM SCHEME

THE GRID IS
EMPHASIZED
WITH EVERY
ELEMENT

This fabulously glamorous room is a harmony of neutral tones and textures — sheer silver curtains, cream linen upholstery and velvet cushion bands, natural and dark wood, glossy lacquer and shiny chrome and glassware.

MONOCHROME

When I'm designing a monochrome interior, the timeless glamour of black-and-white photography always comes to mind. This style of décor is stylish and elegant, yet understated and subtle, creating the perfect backdrop for furniture, furnishings and art.

Perfectly balanced black, white and shades of grey are timelessly elegant.

A monochrome decorating palette is, strictly speaking, composed of shades of only one colour, from light to dark and everything in between. But here I'm referring to interiors where all the decorating components are black, its polar opposite white, and every shade of grey you could create by blending the two colours together in different quantities. The golden rule is never to mix greys with cool and warm undertones: pick one or the other and stick to it.

Monochrome schemes can be light and crisp, or dark and dramatic, depending on whether it's the white and paler silvery greys that dominate or the black and charcoal end of the spectrum. The finished effect is also influenced by the materials and textures you choose. Lots of reflective surfaces – shiny marble, glossy lacquer, silvery metals, such as chrome, and glass, crystal and mirror – will produce a very different feel from a plethora of matt wood, stone, plaster and paintwork, light-absorbing fabrics, such as suede and flat velvet, and dark metals, such as bronze and iron.

A monochrome scheme lends itself to layering textures – here, high-gloss marble and lacquer, leather, and matt velvet and linen.

MONOCHROME SCHEMES

Black wood for the floor and joinery, with runners of limestone, marble or grey wood with brass inlays; wall runners in stone, marble or wood; linen upholstery; textures and sheers for curtains, mixed fabrics for soft furnishings; lacquered tables.

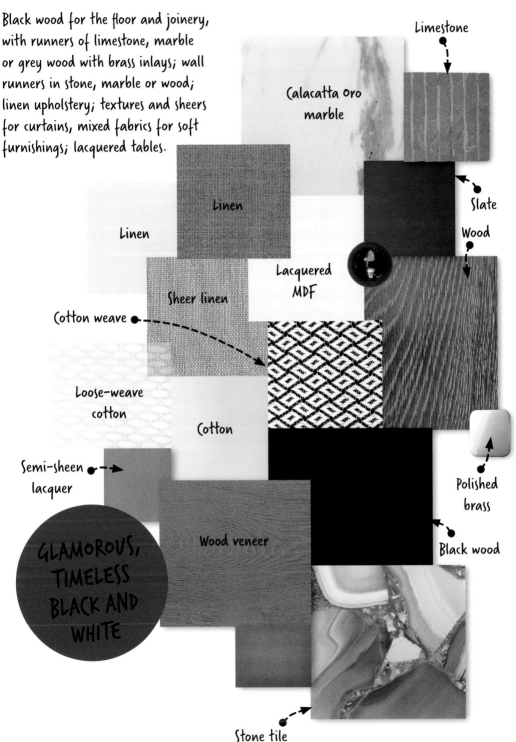

Limestone

Calacatta oro marble

Slate

Linen

Wood

Linen

Lacquered MDF

Sheer linen

Cotton weave

Loose-weave cotton

Cotton

Semi-sheen lacquer

Polished brass

GLAMOROUS, TIMELESS BLACK AND WHITE

Wood veneer

Black wood

Stone tile

TAUPE

I'm known for my love of taupe and for me it really is the most perfect neutral, being neither too warm nor too cool but the ideal balance. Taupe schemes tend to produce rooms that are welcoming, calming and supremely stylish.

Taupe has been my go-to neutral for more than forty years of designing interiors, and that's because I love the serene ambience it creates and how that makes me feel. When you walk into a taupe room, it is instantly warm and welcoming, but also elegant and sophisticated. Equally importantly, a taupe room scheme is sufficiently understated so as not to detract from the art, furniture and personal collections that give a space the stamp of your personality.

This easy-to-live-with colour is at its most tranquil when used tone on tone, with a fabulous mix of tactile textures, materials and finishes layered together to create interest and depth. Taupe can also be combined with whites and creams for a lighter, fresher look, or paired with shades of grey, black or dark wood for a more moody atmosphere. Just make sure you stick to only warm or cool undertones, and never mix the two.

Clear glass and Perspex, chrome, nickel and bronze are all easy companions for a taupe scheme, while deep red, berry tones and rich browns make striking accents.

Taupe wood, walls, carpet and furnishings create a hallway of understated elegance.

This bedroom-cum-living room is both sophisticated and cocooning, thanks to the tonal layering of silk carpet, linen, velvet, silk, suede and leather, with black and metal accents.

TAUPE SCHEMES

Wood floors with marble detailing; specialist plaster for walls or wall runners; leather for upholstery; nickel door furniture; cane chairs; and accents of ceramic and milk glass.

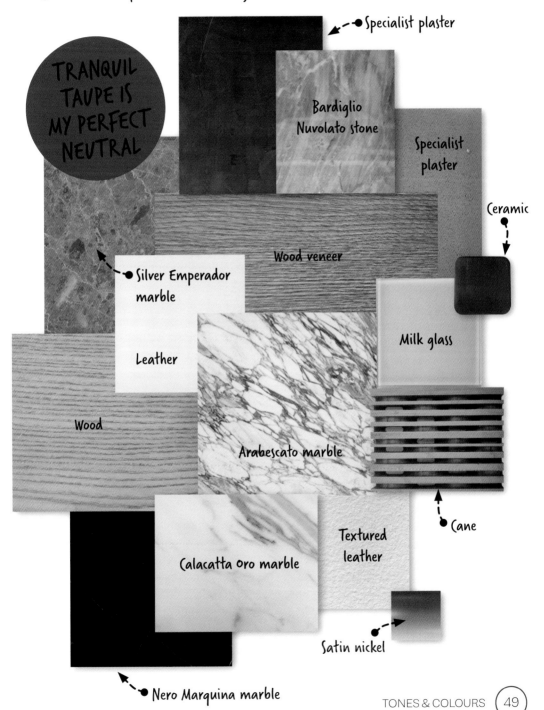

Specialist plaster

TRANQUIL TAUPE IS MY PERFECT NEUTRAL

Bardiglio Nuvolato stone

Specialist plaster

Ceramic

Wood veneer

Silver Emperador marble

Milk glass

Leather

Wood

Arabescato marble

Cane

Calacatta oro marble

Textured leather

Satin nickel

Nero Marquina marble

EARTHY TONES

From the warm shades of sand to the
rich, deep colours of clay and soil, there
is something honest and grounding
about earthy tones when they are used
in interiors, which is perhaps due to their
associations with nature.

The Rock occasional table
adds gold glamour to this
earthy living room scheme.

Nature is known to have a balancing and
soothing effect on us, so perhaps that is part of
the appeal of this family of colours, which has its
roots in the natural world. Natural companions
for this colour scheme are organic materials,
such as wood, sisal, linen and stone, along with
bronze, gold and mother-of-pearl, which are
perfect foils for the earthiness and add a touch of
welcome glamour. Earthy tones are comfortable
with black and white, while accent colours should
be chosen to enhance the richness of this palette –
think burnt orange, rusty reds and verdigris.

I often use this family of neutrals in rooms that have
a traditional or masculine feel, such as studies and
libraries, which seem to lend themselves to materials
such as leather, suede and natural polished wood.
Earthy tones also work well for living spaces in
colder climates, where they engender a feeling of
warmth, especially with the addition of a roaring fire,
glowing lamps creating pools of light, and sumptuous
faux-fur rugs, velvet cushions and wool throws.

Lighting can be used to
enhance or create colour.
Here, LED strips light these
shelves from underneath,
bathing them in a warm
golden glow.

At the paler end of the spectrum, warm sandy
tones can look wonderful in lighter, summery
spaces. Team them with fresh white, buttery
creams, gold-coloured wood, and linens, marble
or stone with yellowy undertones.

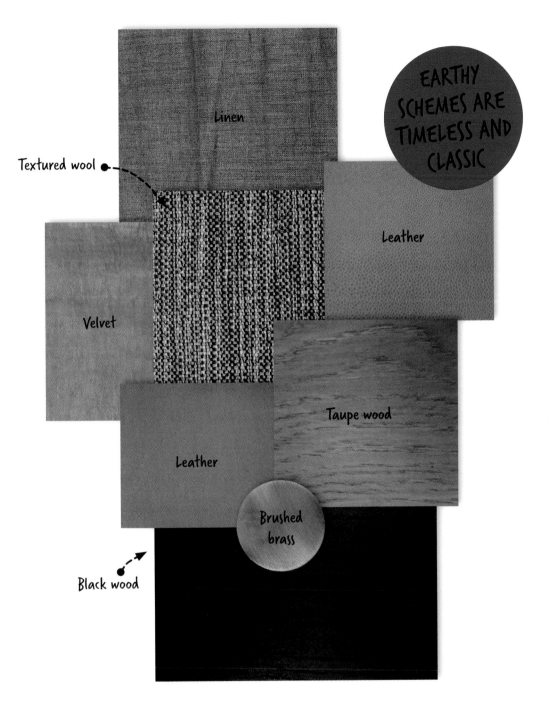

Linen

Textured wool

Velvet

Leather

Taupe wood

Leather

Brushed brass

Black wood

EARTHY SCHEMES ARE TIMELESS AND CLASSIC

EARTHY SCHEMES

Black wood for floors with runners and joinery in taupe wood
with brushed brass for inlaid detail and door furniture;
upholstery in a rich mix of leathers, linen, velvet and wool.

BALANCED NEUTRALS

The art of creating a harmonious interior is to compose a decorating scheme with a balanced mix of light, mid- and dark tones that all sit comfortably together. Make sure that within that range there are a variety of textures at play.

This principle can apply to designing tone-on-tone schemes in just one colour family or in a range of complementary neutrals, such as cream, taupe and dark chocolate, for example, or white, grey and black. The key is to select a mix of materials, finishes and fabrics that all have either warm or cool undertones; this will ensure they sit together comfortably.

In schemes such as these, neither dark nor light dominates, but throughout the space there is a calming mix of both, where each balances out the other. The mid-tones that fall between the two extremes bridge the gap in equal measure, so that although when you look closely there are dramatic contrasts at play, the overall picture is soothing and seamless, and the space is comfortable to be in.

A balanced neutral scheme can be especially successful in an open-plan space, as you can repeat tones and textures in the different zones but with a slightly different emphasis in each. For example, a taupe carpet in one area might be echoed by taupe upholstery in another.

Layers of texture, balanced tones and a pop of yellow create a warm bedroom.

The dining room is linked to the living area by the considered balance of light and dark on the floors and walls, with the dark velvet runners on the taupe upholstery echoing the dark wooden beams, slats and shelf that define the design grid.

Bouclé

THE PERFECT MIX OF LIGHT AND DARK

Satin brass

Textured leather

Textured leather

Linen

Taupe veneer

White onyx

Black timber

Panda stone

BALANCED NEUTRAL SCHEMES

Flooring with runner details in Panda stone or white onyx with black timber; taupe veneer sideboard or storage unit; leather, bouclé and linen upholstery; pendant lights with brass detail.

DARK & RICH

Nothing can beat a deep, dark colour palette in a mix of rich, sumptuous, tactile textures for creating drama and atmosphere. This is the ultimate statement décor and will really pack a punch when done well.

Rich, moody colours work brilliantly in rooms that are mainly used at night, where they create a cosy, enveloping feeling. Shades of black, charcoal and bitter chocolate make spaces such as bedrooms and TV or media rooms feel warm and nurturing. Formal dining areas will look chic and theatrical, while the addition of lots of crystal, silverware and candlelight will ensure they also feel intimate and romantic. Even a cloakroom can be transformed into a glamorous small space when decorated in this deep colour palette.

In such rooms, carefully thought-out lighting is essential to enhance the quality of the different materials and finishes, and to ensure the space feels welcoming rather than gloomy. Crystal or silver statement lights will add enchanting sparkle, while soft pools of light from lamps will create an inviting ambience, and washes of light across the floor or walls from uplights or downlights will highlight textures.

Light-reflecting surfaces will add softness and charm to these deep tones. Think of polished dark wood, gleaming lacquer and the sheen of silk and velvet, along with silver or chrome, crystal, glass, Perspex and mother-of-pearl.

Damask is a great fabric for introducing subtle pattern.

Silk velvet cushions add a tactile quality to a damask-upholstered sofa.

Mother-of-pearl buttons shine against chocolate velvet.

DARK & RICH SCHEMES

Dark grey wood with Viola marble for floors; lacquered MDF joinery; doors in black veneer with stainless-steel door furniture; linen and leather furnishings.

Lacquered MDF

Textured leather

Leather

Linen sheer

Linen

DARK TONES AND RICH TEXTURES ADD DRAMA

Textured leather

Linen

Stainless steel

Viola marble

Linen

Dark grey wood

Black veneer

ACCENT COLOURS – PERFECT COMBINATIONS

Contrary to what many people think, I'm by no means allergic to colour and I love the extra dimension that cleverly selected accents can bring to a space. Used in the right way, colour accents inject instant energy and vitality.

As a rule, less is more when you are introducing accent colours. One well-chosen colour that complements your scheme, creates the right mood for the space in question, and reflects your personality and sense of fun will have far greater impact than three different hues scattered throughout.

Colour accents don't have to be bold. This dusty-pink chest with silver detailing is soft and feminine against the pale grey wall.

An accent colour may be strong and vibrant or soft and subtle, but whether it is chosen to make a bold statement or quietly pull the scheme together, the way it completely changes the look and ambience of a room never fails to delight me.

Colour accents can be expressed in the more permanent elements of a room, such as the edging or trim on a carpet, a star piece of furniture, or a stripe in the curtain or upholstery fabric. In this case, you need to be very sure you love it and that it has the desired effect. Alternatively, you can introduce accents in more transient ways, such as cut flowers, art or objects that are displayed on rotation, or soft furnishings that are changed with the seasons.

AN UNEXPECTED
BURST OF COLOUR

COLOUR ACCENTS ADD NEW ENERGY

In an elegant interior decorated in neutral tones, a pop of bold, bright colour on the inside of a cupboard or cabinet is a joyful surprise every time the doors are opened.

White, monochrome and pale neutral interiors are fairly easygoing about their colour companions – most colours work, as long as you choose the right tone to complement your scheme as a whole. Bold accents such as red and brown look striking, while shades of green and blue are particular favourites of mine for their soothing effect, perhaps because of their connotations with growing natural elements – grass, leaves and shoots – and the sea and sky. From soft seafoam or muted khaki, to vibrant moss or turquoise, to deepest emerald or navy, these colours work well with natural materials, organic shapes and metals – iron, bronze, brass, chrome and nickel.

A bowl of glossy green limes on a Calacatta marble bar-top with polished brass inlays looks fresh and vibrant while waiting to be added to drinks.

ORGANIC ELEMENTS BREATHE LIFE INTO A SPACE

The soft pink buds and aquamarine ceramic vases are striking against the white backdrop.

The soft blue-green linen of the headboard is used as a trim on the bed cover, adding soothing colour to this pale neutral bedroom.

Bring the outdoors in. Evergreen echeveria plants are displayed on a bed of moss in shallow nickel bowls on a white-lacquered coffee table.

The colours tone and the textures contrast as soft flower heads stand out against the specialist textured and coloured plaster finish.

Cream walls, floors, upholstery or soft furnishings are perfectly partnered with the mellow tones of rich, dark, bitter chocolate, earthy browns and black. Warm taupe, if it has a complementary undertone, can be used in small doses – as cushion bands or runners in a contrasting texture, for example – to add tonal depth, or in larger expanses, such as flooring or upholstery, to create a more balanced neutral scheme. Using unusual fabrics in unexpected ways – perhaps parachute silk for curtains, or metal studs, chain mail or webbing as a trim – can give your furniture and furnishings a unique spin.

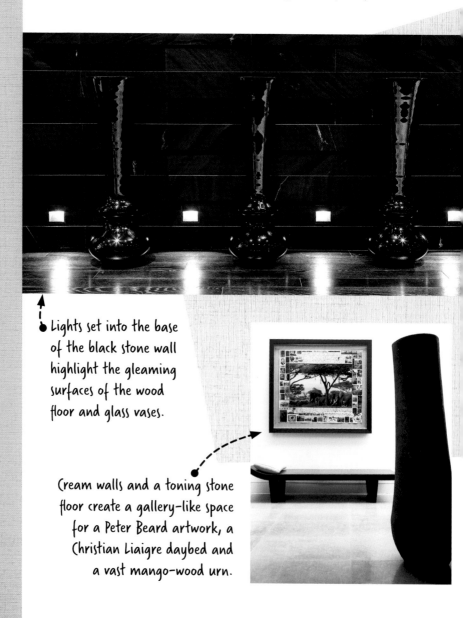

Lights set into the base of the black stone wall highlight the gleaming surfaces of the wood floor and glass vases.

Cream walls and a toning stone floor create a gallery-like space for a Peter Beard artwork, a Christian Liaigre daybed and a vast mango-wood urn.

A Baltus chair with an unusual black frame and embroidered silk upholstery is an object of beauty against a pale taupe carpet, smoky glass and cream walls.

Glamorous Fortuny pleated silk in rich chocolate trails on dark parquet flooring.

Vintage chairs, reinvented with black leather and studs, create impact with bronze and glass in a cream setting.

GIVE FURNITURE
A TWIST WITH
UNEXPECTED
FABRICS AND TRIMS

Warm, yellow-based neutrals fall into the sand colour range and encompass everything from pale gold-beige shades to richer, deeper honey hues. These neutrals have an earthy, organic appeal and work well with toning wood, stone, leather and suede. White, cream and small amounts of black make a striking contrast, while caramel, toffee, rust, coffee and burnt orange add depth to a sand scheme. Warm-coloured metals, such as brass, bronze, copper and gold, are great choices for introducing shiny textures to play against the matt finish of painted walls, the natural grain of wood and the weave of linen.

Painting the shelved alcoves orange is a striking way to add colour to an elegant pale sand dining space.

Brass strips, set into the sand-toned veneer of the built-in bedside table, are replaced by backlit strips as the runner extends up the wall.

Sand-veneer niches and black-lacquered doors create a chequerboard effect.

An orange-lacquered desk, rug and flowers tone with the honey-coloured wood floor and the sand linen seat of the Perspex chair.

This stunning stained-beech cabinet with silver-plated bronze flower studs, by Garouste and Bonetti, is the star piece in this simple pale sand and white room.

Metallic accents bring glamour to any space. This egg-shaped chest of drawers in silver-plated bronze by Garouste and Bonetti offsets the hard lines of this space.

TONING AND SUBTLE ACCENTS WORK BETTER WITH SAND THAN BOLD CONTRASTS

Calming, elegant taupe schemes can be grounded by touches of black, freshened by white, and warmed and energized by splashes of red. From bright scarlet and crimson to deep burgundy, port and berry tones, red accents work in all fabrics and materials, from leather, velvet and linen to lacquer, glass and flowers. Taupe with red and black gives a nod to the East-meets-West aesthetic that I love and is one of my signature colour combinations, often with the addition of white. It works as well in contemporary, clean-lined spaces as it does in traditional homes with architectural features and natural materials.

A red-and-white wall-mounted shelf, alongside the black joinery, turn this wall into a graphic statement reminiscent of modern art.

A Perspex tray of red dahlia heads creates impact on a black tabletop.

An antique reproduction chair by Massant, upholstered in bold crimson leather, adds glamour to a taupe room.

Scarlet velvet makes an unexpectedly luxe contrast with taupe linen, carpet and wood cladding.

Balancing light and dark, the taupe hall is accented by gold, crystal, wrought iron and indigo lacquer.

A black-lacquered coffee table looks striking against a red and taupe striped rug.

TAUPE WITH BLACK AND RED IS ONE OF MY FAVOURITE COLOUR COMBINATIONS

TEXTURE

In my rulebook, texture is everything and can make or break a design. Any room that doesn't have a variety of contrasting textures at play, complementing, balancing and enhancing each other's qualities, will seem bland and boring.

Building up layers of texture throughout any room scheme creates interest, depth and character. Composing the perfect mix, where everything is in balance and proportion, takes time and consideration but can mean the difference between a space that feels flat and dull and one that feels inviting and inspiring. Layers of texture add that extra wow factor and are the best way to elevate a room to a place where there is something to feed and delight all the senses.

CREATING A TEXTURAL STORY

Texture is something to consider at every level, from the key components of the floor and wall finishes, fittings, furniture and soft furnishings – especially the choice of textiles – to the finishing touches of art, objects and accessories. Even details such as door handles, decorative trims and embellishments on cushions should be taken into account, as they all contribute to the overall picture that defines the mood of a room.

Texture cannot be considered separately from colour: the two are inextricably linked, because how a colour looks depends on how light is absorbed or reflected by it, which in turn depends on the texture of the surface in question. The same colour will appear very different in matt and glossy finishes, for example – think of a glossy white ceramic tile alongside chalky white paintwork, or a chocolate suede ottoman on a polished dark wood floor, a taupe silk velvet cushion on a taupe linen sofa.

This is why it is so crucial to create a material board for each room you are designing. You'll need to gather lots of samples in colours, materials and finishes you're drawn to, and then play around with them to see which combination works best and gives you the effect you're looking for.

PROPORTION IS EVERYTHING

Remember that a colour or finish will look very different from the small square on your board when it is covering a large expanse – on the walls or floor, for example. Decide on the colours and textures for these large expanses first, as they will be the most dominant in your scheme. Then build up the textural picture over the rest of the elements. Have no more than two or three dominant textures and then add accent layers to create depth.

Hard and soft textures are at play here, with a sumptuous shaggy black goatskin rug acting as a counterpoint to the strong lines and smooth surfaces of the black leather and chrome seating. Note the different effects of the light as it lands on each material.

CREATE CONTRASTS

The textural mix you choose for each room will help to engender its mood, whether warm, enveloping and sensuous or cool, clean-lined and practical. Either way, texture is intrinsically linked to colour and form so these elements must be considered together.

CHOOSE MATERIALS TO DELIGHT THE SENSES

As well as making a room look more interesting, different textures appeal to other senses, too. Think about how flooring sounds when you walk on it – as you move over bare floorboards onto carpet, for example – or the seductive rustle of silk taffeta curtains when you open and close them. Think of the softness as you sink onto voluptuous velvet sofa cushions, the warm embrace of a cashmere throw on a chilly evening, or the cool smoothness of a polished stone floor under bare feet. Ultimately, the mix of textures you choose for your home should be informed as much by delighting these senses as by what looks good together. This is what ensures that the design of a home is truly multidimensional, where there is something to appeal and enhance the experience at every level.

JUXTAPOSITIONS

The art of good design is to find a collection of colours and textures – for walls, floors, furniture, furnishings, accessories and art – that work well together. By that I mean they should either complement each other or contrast with each other, and sit harmoniously together, with neither one competing

A polished-marble-effect surfboard complements the matt veneer door with dark, linear detailing.

I designed this kitchen unit for Smallbone. The carcass is made from glossy taupe lacquer, which looks sleek and modern, but the unexpected twist is the chain-mail curtains that hang from each shelf, elevating the simple white ceramic bowls into works of art.

for attention at the expense of the other, so the overall effect is balanced. This is why it's important to choose materials for the larger expanses carefully and consider how dominant they will seem within the finished room.

The idea of juxtaposing contrasting textures is to emphasize and enhance the qualities and characteristics of each. A silk velvet cushion will seem to have even more depth and sheen against natural linen upholstery; a chrome door handle will shine brighter against dark-stained wood; and a crystal wall light will sparkle all the more against a chalky matt paint finish.

SOFT, HARD
COOL, WARM
SMOOTH, ROUGH

Throughout all my designs, I work to create a visual interaction between strong, hard lines and soft, sensuous curves, as this brings a sense of movement, energy and balance to a space. Curves are the 'yang' to the 'yin' of straight lines and hard edges, and add a sense of comfort and softness.

The most obvious straight lines are invariably the architectural framework of a room – the doors, ceilings, walls, floor and support columns or beams. They may also be picture frames, shelves, steps, the outline of a window shutter or blind, or linear furniture. Curves may be furniture or architectural features, lighting, a sweeping staircase, vases or sculptures.

The strong verticals and horizontals of the design grid are evident here, offset by the curves of the lighting and furniture.

I hung these oversized 'floating' glass bubbles, from DARK, in shades that I designed in my living area. Their curves reflect the light and counterbalance the linear elements.

FORM, COLOUR AND TEXTURE GO HAND IN HAND

A sculptural shelf, 'Dune 01' (2007), by Zaha Hadid (Editions David Gill, London).

In this open-plan space, the strong lines of the architecture and the natural and lacquered flooring that defines the zones are interrupted by curved components, including the silver-lacquered resin floating shelf and the row of cylindrical vases.

ORGANIC SHAPES & MATERIALS

I have always loved using organic shapes and materials in the homes I design. They bring a certain authenticity, integrity and calming energy to a space. Nature has a very grounding, soothing effect and there is something undeniably pleasing about the natural grain of wood, the veined patterns of marble, the delicate-looking yet rock-hard formations of farmed coral and the magical contours of quartz and crystal.

I also love creating simple displays of fresh flowers, choosing the blooms to accent the colour scheme of each room. Trays or dishes of succulents and moss are another easy way to introduce an additional element of texture and colour into the mix.

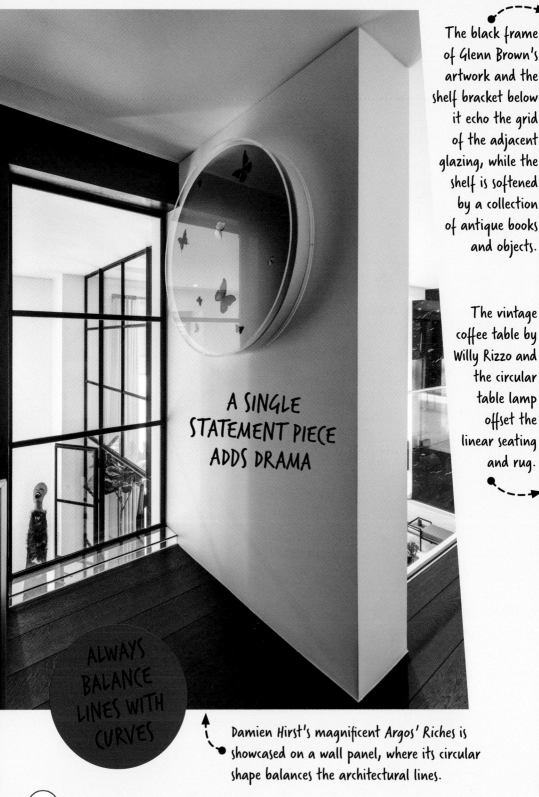

The black frame of Glenn Brown's artwork and the shelf bracket below it echo the grid of the adjacent glazing, while the shelf is softened by a collection of antique books and objects.

The vintage coffee table by Willy Rizzo and the circular table lamp offset the linear seating and rug.

A SINGLE STATEMENT PIECE ADDS DRAMA

ALWAYS BALANCE LINES WITH CURVES

Damien Hirst's magnificent Argos' Riches is showcased on a wall panel, where its circular shape balances the architectural lines.

When you're introducing smooth curves and organic shapes to offset straight lines, it's important to create a comfortable balance so the overall effect is harmonious. Think about the structure of the room first of all – the position and proportions of the doors, windows and fireplace, and any built-in joinery or shelving. Then think about ways to bring in curves and organic elements to act as foils. This could be in the form of statement door furniture, a patterned or artfully draped window treatment, or circular mirrors, pictures or clocks on the wall. It could also be pieces of furniture with sensuous curves or organic shapes or materials, or sculptures, ornaments, vases, crystals or coral displayed on shelves or tabletops.

FURNITURE

Sofas and beds tend to be linear, so think about counterbalancing their lines with bolster cushions, circular tables or stools, a curved headboard or chairs, or with organic-shaped lighting or mirrors. If your coffee table is square or rectangular, for example, redress its hard lines with a curved dish, vase or display of flowers.

DECORATIVE OBJECTS

Farmed or resin coral, crystals and quartz, and glass vases of flowers or foliage are some of my favourite items to display. Ceramics, sculptures, art and statement lighting are other easy ways to introduce sensuous curves and organic shapes.

Three tall glass cylinders of bamboo stems add a natural element and a pop of green to an eclectic display on a shelf.

Texture is a vital ingredient when defining the mood of a room, especially in the cases of rough and smooth, and hard and soft. Decisions on texture can set the tone of a space, whether it's sleek and contemporary, with expanses of glass, chrome or marble; traditional and elegant, with a comfortable mix of natural wood, leather and antiques; rustic and timeworn, with stone flags, warm rugs and linen textiles; or industrial and modern, with stretches of polished concrete, mesh screens and Perspex furniture. Practicality should also be a key factor in your decision-making process, as every material must be fit for purpose. It's essential to consider durability, application cost and upkeep.

Linen mesh curtains behind a row of three black-lacquered urns enhance their smooth, shiny contours.

Layers of texture create interest and a sense of luxury — a white silk-and-linen carpet edged with black faux-crocodile adds softness to a grey stone floor.

REPETITION CREATES IMPACT

A simple collection of black ceramic tea caddies creates an effective contrast with the traditional carved marble fireplace.

TACTILITY

I always take a holistic approach to design, organically building up a picture that pulsates with life and soul and is pleasing to all the senses. Tactility is key. Surfaces should make you want to run your fingers over them or sink your toes into them.

How you use textures can also imbue a room with a sense of cosiness and warmth or crisp coolness. Imagine the experience of entering a room that has an expanse of polished stone tiles compared to one with deep-pile carpet, or one that's furnished with sleek leather and chrome seating as opposed to enveloping armchairs with cushions upholstered in brushed linen.

Shaggy sheepskin on silk carpet is the ultimate treat for bare feet.

A traditional material can be given an unexpected twist, such as this slashed and frayed linen scrim blind, juxtaposed with a glossy wood sill and damask upholstery.

THINK OUTSIDE THE BOX

Creative juxtapositions are what make interior schemes sing, adding an unexpected frisson to a design that takes it beyond the mundane. When you are compiling your material board, always look for new and unusual ways to mix things up and create arresting contrasts. Remember, opposing textures will always exaggerate the effect of each – a coarse linen curtain trimmed with silk, a rustic wooden bowl displayed on a smooth lacquered shelf, or an exposed brick wall adjacent to one of polished plaster. These are some of my favourite eye-catching pairings, but I also like to experiment with other materials to create surprising and interesting textural details, such as using chain mail as a fringe or a curtain, rows of brass studs to create runners on a leather floor, or strips of coarse upholstery webbing as a trim for sheer curtains.

APPLICATION

Textural contrasts may be achieved on a large scale, such as smooth marble flooring juxtaposed with a rough stone wall, or a sisal carpet running up a staircase with a glass balustrade and

This fabulous trilogy of contrasting textures is typical of the combinations I put together – a Monpas folding metal mesh screen in front of open-weave curtains draping onto a chic blackened wood floor.

MAKE THE MOST OF EXISTING FEATURES

I hung chain mail at the kitchen window of a previous home of mine, a former school. The hundreds of metal spheres reflected energy back into the room, which had a positive effect on the whole atmosphere of the space.

Natural wood doors and flooring provide an earthy contrasting backdrop for the smoke-coloured polycarbonate Pedrali armchair with taupe velvet cushion.

sleek wooden handrail. But layering contrasting textures together can also be played out at a much subtler level and on a smaller scale. Every detail counts towards the overall textural picture, from a mesh curtain pooling onto polished floorboards to smooth ceramics against a textured plaster wall, or a coarse natural linen cushion on a Perspex chair.

EXISTING FEATURES

When considering the overall look you want to achieve and the individual mood you want to create in each space, first assess the room as it stands. Take into account any surfaces or features that you want to incorporate, such as a marble fireplace or original floorboards.

Matt and shiny textures are pleasing to include in an interior scheme because they each have very different properties with regards to light. When either natural or artificial light hits a matt surface, it will be absorbed by it, while light landing on a glossy surface is bounced off. This has the effect of increasing the amount of light in a room, which is why mirrors are often used as a device for brightening up dark spaces. It can also create interesting plays of light and shadow, throwing patterns onto adjacent surfaces and adding drama. With their almost mirror-like quality, shiny materials such as metal, glass and lacquer also add visual interest in the form of the reflections of nearby objects and room-scape views that can be seen on their surfaces.

Some of my favourite matt-and-shiny combinations are:

- Mirrors on a chalky painted wall.

- Textured plaster with a contrasting runner of polished plaster or marble.

- A lacquered table on a wood floor.

- A mother-of-pearl or horn button on a linen or velvet cushion.

- A nickel or brass runner set into wood.

Patterns of light and shadow are reflected onto the pale grey textured plaster wall by the mirrored mosaic tiles on the frame of a mirror.

Glossy charcoal mosaics contrast with soft grey patterned matt stone tiles.

MATT AND GLOSS
HAVE DIFFERENT
EFFECTS ON LIGHT

PLAYS OF LIGHT AND SHADOW ADD DRAMA

Delicate strands of chain mail cascade from a pendant light onto the shiny surface of a lacquered tabletop, while a trio of metallic vases create interesting reflections of this off-white and taupe space.

A curtain of chain mail hangs from beneath a shiny, reflective faux mantelpiece. The specialist plaster finish on the wall adds another layer of texture.

METALLICS

Perhaps the most glamorous way to introduce shiny materials into a room scheme is with metallics. Whether the warm glint of a gilt picture frame, a gold-leaf finish or nickel door furniture, the subtle gleam of a dark bronze side table or wrought-iron handrail, the bold statement of a copper lamp shade or brass tap, or the cool silver finish of shiny chrome trim or inset runners, dashes of metal complement an interior like well-chosen jewellery completes an outfit. Metallics don't compete with other shiny elements, such as lacquer or glass, and look wonderful against matt surfaces.

A trio of glossy black-lacquered Flibuste tables by Christian Liaigre makes an impact on a textured silk carpet reminiscent of a raked Zen garden. The glass jars of moss add another layer of texture.

A mesh curtain pools on a shiny polished stone floor juxtaposed with taupe carpet.

LAYERS OF MATT AND SHINY ADD INTEREST

Contrasting shiny and matt materials in the form of runners are a great way to emphasize the design grid.

Antiquarian books in glass cases seem to float against the textured plaster walls.

A taupe wood floor is inlaid with a strip of shiny chrome that draws the eye up the steps and along the passage. The walls are clad in padded linen panels separated by dark wood runners.

Using transparent and opaque materials within a room scheme allows you to manipulate and filter light, and to play with solidity and shadows. See-through materials allow uninterrupted vistas and have a certain weightless quality. Translucent materials diffuse light softly, blurring the edges and creating a feeling of warmth, whereas opaque surfaces deflect light, acting as a barrier to it and casting shadows. Using a balanced mix of transparent and opaque, weightless and solid, can breathe life into a scheme, as it allows energy to flow freely. The only proviso is to make sure the materials you choose are suitable for the room's use and the mood you want to create there.

Transparent acrylic chairs counterbalance the white-painted oak trestle table.

Against the solidity of the dark wood cupboards behind it, the glass Ghost chair, by Cini Boeri for Fiam, seems weightless on the silk carpet.

The hand-blown glass bubbles of this Melogranoblu pendant light appear to float against the linen curtain behind, the spherical, shiny surface sparkling where light hits it.

Clear glass vases sit in chrome-trimmed niches in an off-white lacquered wood display unit.

THE FLOW OF LIGHT

The interplay of light and shadow on solid surfaces creates subtle pattern, depth and drama, which all contribute to the overall atmosphere of a space. Depending on your plans for the room, for the windows you might choose wooden plantation shutters with slats that can be opened to varying degrees to allow slivers of light in, or closed to create a solid barrier. Alternatively, heavy, lined linen or velvet drapes keep a room cosy, while mesh, cut-out or sheer curtains are unobtrusive and softly diffuse the natural light.

If the space can accommodate it, I love a show-stopper of a glass chandelier, an oversized glass pendant or a cascade of glass bubbles or spheres. Such lights are star pieces even before they are lit.

This type of textural contrast can be introduced into a home in so many creative ways – from window treatments, light fittings, furniture, shelving, display units and accessories to certain structural and architectural elements. In the same way that your choice of window treatment determines the amount and strength of natural light that can enter the space, the materials you choose for walls, doors, room dividers, screens and balustrades – even flooring – can either allow light to flow freely through them or provide a more solid boundary. The choice is endless, from clear, sand-blasted, etched or milk glass to transparent or coloured Perspex, metal mesh or glass bricks. Materials can be selected to create seamless or partial boundaries that don't block the light, or that filter, tint or diffuse it softly, or that retain privacy while still allowing borrowed light to flow freely between adjacent spaces.

FLOATING FURNITURE

Clear glass, Perspex and acrylic furniture – tables, chairs and stools – have a sense of weightlessness that almost makes them appear to float. This barely-there quality means such unobtrusive pieces are a good choice for smaller spaces, where heavier items could dominate or overwhelm. Clear shelves or display units also seem to float and allow whatever is on them to take centre stage.

Transparent furniture is also shiny and light-reflecting. As such, it counterbalances heavy, solid pieces; contrasts with both rough and matt textures, including carpet, wood and linen; and also works in juxtaposition with glossy lacquer and metal.

ON A SMALL SCALE

Introduce contrasts of transparency and opacity on a small scale, too, with details such as glass doorknobs or curtain finials. Collections of glassware can contribute great personality, colour or texture to a room, while even simple vases, thoughtfully displayed, can be elevated into objects of striking beauty.

Like a crystal ball, a solid glass sphere on an oak newel post reflects the staircase and chandelier above.

CLEAR GLASS OR ACRYLIC PIECES WORK IN MOST SPACES

Contemporary interpretations of the iconic mid-century Bubble chair by Eero Aarnio are some of my favourite pieces of furniture for adding organic curves and light-reflecting transparency.

FLOORS & WALLS

Both walls and floors offer enormous scope for introducing contrasting textures and materials into a room scheme. These surfaces cover large expanses, so the key thing is to decide whether you want them to recede into the background or make a statement.

When you are making decisions about flooring and wall treatments, take into account the proportions of the room, the position of doors, windows and architectural features, and your design grid. Runners along the floor and up or along walls are excellent ways to emphasize the grid, while at the same time introducing a new material, pattern or texture. Also consider the furniture and art and make sure that whatever you choose for the flooring and walls will complement rather than compete with these elements. If the budget is tight, a feature wall or runner offers the opportunity to use a small quantity of a more expensive material.

HAKWOOD X KELLY HOPPEN
I'm not known for my use of pattern but I'm thrilled with my collection of wood wall and floor tiles, which I designed for the Dutch company Hakwood. The six interchangeable tile designs, available in four colourways – combinations of my signature tones of black, white and taupe – can be used in many different configurations to cover walls, floors or sections of either.

If you choose a patterned floor, keep the walls plain, and vice versa.

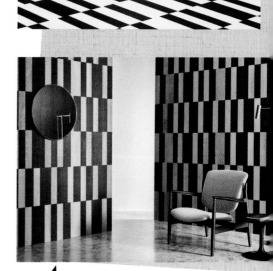

The Grid design in Abstract makes a dramatic statement on either walls or floors. It has a mid-century feel and works well with classic clean-lined furniture from that era.

The Cube design in Abstract has been used on this floor with plain companion tiles.

My collection of wall and floor tiles offers endless design possibilities — bold, graphic, elegant style the easy way.

BOLD, GRAPHIC, VERSATILE AND OH SO CHIC

These versatile wood tiles can be used in small quantities as wall art and still make a large impact. This is the Square design in Iconic.

This graphic floor is the Square design in Bold — so chic and glamorous. This would be an ideal choice for emphasizing the design grid.

MAKE A STATEMENT OR CREATE A FEATURE

FLOORING CONSIDERATIONS

It is usually best to defer your choice of flooring until you have decided on the rest of the design scheme. That way, you can make your decision based on what materials, colours and textures will best complement the wall finishes, window treatments, furniture and furnishings you have selected. Flooring should tie all of these elements together and act as a foundation that will unify the design as a whole.

Hard, soft or a combination of the two is often the first decision to make. Hard flooring, such as stone, marble or resin, may be good choices for a bathroom or kitchen, while a silk carpet that is soft and warm under bare feet is usually appealing in bedrooms where comfort is key. Areas that see heavy traffic, such as stairs or hallways, need to be hard-wearing and fit for purpose. Always take advice from the manufacturer or supplier regarding suitability of use – a floor that stains easily will be an expensive mistake in a kitchen, while one that can't withstand occasional puddles of water is not a good choice for a family bathroom. Also, if you want to install underfloor heating, check that your choice of flooring is appropriate.

ZONING

One of my signature design devices is to use two or more flooring materials or textures adjacent to each other. This is a useful way of designating different zones within an open-plan space – perhaps dark-stained wood for a connecting walkway, with a taupe silk carpet, bordered in a contrasting colour and texture such as burgundy leather, defining a comfy seating area. Or it could be applied in the form of runners that underpin the design grid and draw the eye from one area to the next – taupe wood inlaid with narrow strips of brass, for instance, or blackened wood set into natural limestone or glossy white or taupe lacquer.

When juxtaposing two different flooring materials in this way, it is essential that the installation is done professionally. Anything less than top-quality expert workmanship could result in an uneven finish that will spoil the entire effect and be expensive to rectify.

Flooring is a considerable outlay, so it needs to be timeless, stylish and able to withstand the wear and tear of daily use.

This taupe parquet floor adds subtle pattern, matt texture and warm taupe tones.

Geometric black-and-white marble gives my entrance hall a wow factor.

Narrow strips of brass inlaid between taupe wood boards is a de luxe detail.

Black oak and white resin make a striking monochrome floor. This is one of my favourite combinations.

LIGHTING

Plenty of natural light flooding into the interior is a desirable commodity in any home, as it lifts the mood and works in harmony with the body's circadian rhythms. Artificial light is essential for boosting low levels of daylight, when necessary, but it really comes into its own when evening falls and natural light fades.

Lighting is one of the most important aspects of design and must be given due consideration. It must also be allocated a fair portion of the budget. Lighting is not something to skimp on, as a well-designed lighting scheme will elevate your home like no other element, ensuring it is functional, practical and safe, as well as delivering on ambience and aesthetics. Conversely, inadequate or badly thought-out lighting will make a space feel flat, dull and unwelcoming – not to mention being unflattering to everyone within it.

Installing wiring, sockets and switches, as well as any wall, floor and ceiling light fittings in the numbers and positions you want them, causes a lot of upheaval and can be messy work. For this reason, it needs to be addressed early on in your home's transformation. However, you need to get to a certain point in the design and planning process in order to make those key decisions successfully.

The first step is to familiarize yourself with the space. Observe how the levels and quality of natural light change throughout the day – both when it's sunny and when it isn't. This knowledge may even determine a room's use.

Only then will you be in a position to make decisions about colours, textures, materials and finishes, perhaps deciding to introduce glossy surfaces to reflect natural light. Finally, plan the furniture layout and the positions of key artworks. All these decisions have a direct bearing on the lighting design.

Reflective surfaces in this imposing East-meets-West lobby in Taiwan make the most of natural light filtering through the signature screens by Kelly Hoppen Interiors. This is supplemented by a mix of lighting, including clusters of Tom Dixon's Mirror Ball pendants.

ENHANCE
NATURAL
LIGHT WITH
ARTIFICIAL

TASK LIGHTING

The secret of good lighting design is to build in as much flexibility as possible, with layers of light catering to different needs, each controlled by separate circuits within a space. Task light is the practical element within a lighting scheme.

THIS IS THE FUNCTIONAL LAYER OF LIGHT IN ANY INTERIOR

INTEGRAL LIGHTING IS A GREAT OPTION FOR BUILT-IN UNITS

Task lighting is necessary for carrying out numerous everyday activities, from getting dressed and putting on make-up or shaving in the morning, to cooking, cleaning and reading. This functional layer of light enables such tasks to be undertaken safely, efficiently and conveniently.

This category of practical illumination also includes navigational lighting, such as a light over the front door so you can locate the lock with your key, as well as clearly see the identity of anyone standing outside at night. In addition, it includes lighting on stairs and along corridors, which is essential for safely moving around the house at night.

PRACTICAL CONSIDERATIONS

Task lighting not only needs to be bright enough for you to see what you are doing but also targeted specifically where you need it. A reading light over a bed, for example, must be angled just so, ensuring it hits the page when the book is held in a comfortable position,

This large dressing room houses clothing, footwear and accessories in a combination of open and closed storage, custom-made in dark-stained oak veneer. The rows of shelves for shoes and bags, a generous hanging space and drawers are lit with integral lighting so items can be located with ease.

without disturbing a partner who is trying to sleep or looking at a screen. This is one reason why it's so important to plan the furniture layout before the lighting scheme, so you can work out exactly where spotlights should be recessed and how they need to be angled to give you a beam of light where you want it.

Task light is often delivered by means of recessed spotlights in ceilings, walls or floors, as well as shadow-gap lighting along skirting boards and up staircases, and integral lights within cupboards or other built-in units. You may want lights in enclosed cupboards to be wired in such a way that they switch on automatically when you open the door. Alternatively, have all your task lights within a space wired into the same circuit, so they can be controlled by one switch or preprogrammed setting.

BEDROOMS & DRESSING ROOMS

Whether you have limited storage for your clothes and shoes or the luxury of a separate dressing room with room for bespoke shelving, drawers and a hanging space, being able to see what you've got and find what you need when you're in a hurry is a priority. A good-sized – ideally, full-length – well-lit mirror is also essential.

For many people, if space allows it, a dedicated beauty station where you can conveniently apply make-up and style hair is also a must, with plenty of sockets for hairdryers, straighteners and tongs. Ideally, these sockets should be integrated into enclosed storage, so that all unsightly appliances, tools and products can be hidden away when not in use.

Lighting here should be bright enough to see what you're doing and to ensure accuracy of application, but it should also be flattering and angled so that it doesn't cast dark shadows over your face. An even glow of light from both sides will be infinitely more flattering than a single light source overhead.

Instead of lamps on bedside tables, I love to hang pendant lights beside the bed. This organic Aloe Blossom ceramic example by Jeremy Cole adds texture as well as light.

Bedside lighting is provided by Lee Broom's Mini Crescent pendants, while a row of Chamber Lights at the dressing table are multiplied by their reflection.

For best results, install task lighting that will give you a natural effect that is as close to daylight as possible.

BRING IN THE PROFESSIONALS

If your budget permits it – and especially if you are planning your lighting from scratch – working with a professional lighting consultant should ensure that you end up with an efficient and flexible scheme that meets your needs at every level and enhances your home. At the very least, discuss your requirements at length with your lighting supplier and electrician, who will have the expertise and technical knowledge to offer you the most appropriate solutions.

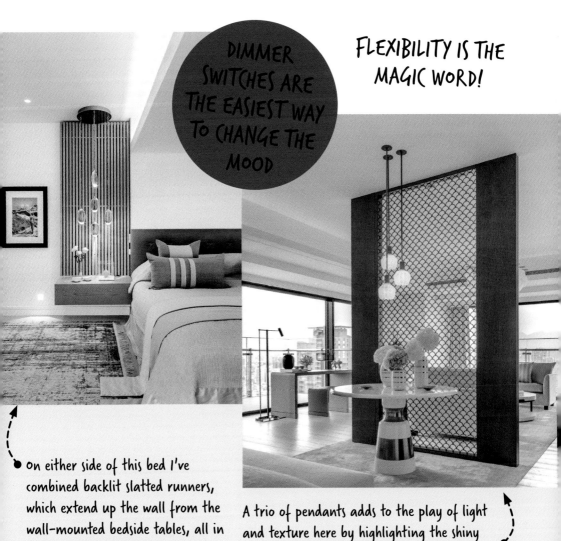

DIMMER SWITCHES ARE THE EASIEST WAY TO CHANGE THE MOOD

FLEXIBILITY IS THE MAGIC WORD!

On either side of this bed I've combined backlit slatted runners, which extend up the wall from the wall-mounted bedside tables, all in taupe wood, with stunning clusters of clear glass pendants.

A trio of pendants adds to the play of light and texture here by highlighting the shiny surface of the table alongside a decorative screen that separates sleeping and living areas.

MOOD LIGHTING

Once the sun has set on the day and the natural light has faded, the overall ambience of any room is dramatically influenced by the type and quality of the lighting. Mood lighting sets the tone of a space, and should be soothing and relaxing.

Clusters of delicate porcelain lights are suspended on each side of the bed, adding soft light and texture, while recessed downlights provide task lighting.

As I've said before, the golden rule for good lighting design is to build up layers of light that will give you as many configurations and options as are practical for the space. Separate circuits and switches that control different combinations of lights within a room will give you the most flexibility, allowing you to light your home as you wish. It also enables you to change the light levels and alter the atmosphere and ambience at the flick of a switch.

Of course, now it's possible to preprogram different lighting 'moods', which can be operated by remote control or through an app on your smart phone. This allows you to have preset combinations of lighting that establish the tone for various activities, such as family suppers, formal dining, parties, relaxed conversation, watching TV or unwinding.

LAYERS OF LIGHT

The practical foundation of a lighting scheme is the task lighting, which allows you to perform everyday activities safely and easily (see page 92). Once you have decided on the type of task light you need in each space, you can begin to incorporate the decorative layers into your design. In addition to general mood lighting, there are accent lights – used to highlight art, displays, architectural features or specialist finishes and textures (see page 100) – and statement lights, which create impact and drama (see page 104).

The alabaster in this steel-framed wall-light-with-mirror diffuses soft light in a tonal bathroom.

POOLS OF LIGHT

Building up layers of light within each space gives you more options, balance and flexibility, with each layer of light having its own role to play as well as working in combination with others, allowing you to create different effects and moods. This gives you maximum control over the level of illumination in your interior, so you can adjust it according to the time of day and the type of activity you are performing.

Mood lighting, as the term suggests, provides the background ambience in a room. Usually the most effective way to achieve this is by creating soft pools of warm light with a mix of table lamps, floor lamps and pendant lights. I like to hang pendants in less predictable

Five identical, simple pendant lights, evenly spaced and hung at the same height, create a soft pool of light.

ways, such as at a low level in the corner of a room or off to the side, or over a seating area or dining table, either singly or in rows or clusters. Soothing washes of light across the walls and floors are also an essential component of mood lighting, with wall lights, uplights and downlights creating a warm background glow.

Bespoke Fortuny lights hang in splendour next to a specialist gold and black plaster finish.

Wall, floor, pendant and hidden lighting all have a part to play in creating balanced pools and washes of light where you need them. Start with a statement light, such as the trio of Cargo pendants by Hervé Langlais, and choose the other lighting elements to complement it.

A floating canopy of silk pendant lights by Fortuny appear delicate and ethereal against the dark timber wall finish.

ACCENT LIGHTING

The purpose of accent lighting is to illuminate displays of objects or art, highlight architectural features and enhance specialist wall and floor finishes and textures. It's what adds the finishing touches to all these elements.

As with all lighting design, before you can plan the accent lighting for your space, you need to have made all the key design decisions about the materials and finishes you are intending to use and the basic layout of your furniture. This includes knowing where art is going to be hung on the walls, and where you are going to display collections on open shelves or in cabinets. This way, wiring can be completed and provisions made for wall, floor or ceiling lights, as necessary, before expensive flooring is laid and wall finishes are applied.

PRECISION IS ESSENTIAL

For best results, it is not enough to know roughly where accent lights will be called for. A professional lighting designer will need a detailed elevation plan of each wall, showing the height and dimensions of the object, feature or collection to be highlighted. They will then be able to assess the type of accent lighting required and, in the case of uplights, downlights and spotlights, calculate the precise angle and width of beam needed.

Hidden lighting dramatizes the outline of this staircase against a bespoke plaster wall finish.

66

Planning accent lighting is a little like painting with beams of light.

99

ARCHITECTURAL LIGHTING

A key component of the overall design, architectural lighting emphasizes the lines of a room and defines the design grid, helping to alter proportions, if necessary. It can also accentuate the form of a staircase, or draw focus onto features such as arches, period details, and alcoves and niches with backlighting. Shadow-gap lighting at floor or ceiling level, or up a staircase, creates a sleek, contemporary effect, while concealed LED strips along the underside of shelves is a less expensive but striking option.

The grid-like doors of this built-in display unit allow tantalizing glimpses through the taupe wood slats of the objects within, lit from above by concealed strip lights.

The hanging sculpture by Jean-Michel Othoniel brings colour and organic shape into the dramatic hallway, while drawing the eye upwards.

LIGHTING IS INTEGRAL TO THE OVERALL DESIGN

Architectural lighting usually refers to indirect lighting, where the light source itself is not seen – for example, LED shadow-gap lighting along skirting boards and stairs; LED strip lights or recessed downlights on the underside of shelves or cabinets; or lighting concealed within a ceiling recess or light coffer. Here, it is the light effect that creates the drama, rather than the light itself – the opposite of statement lighting, where the light fitting is the star of the show. This light effect could be a warm glow from beneath built-in joinery, which makes it appear almost weightless, as though it is floating, or a soft glow above fitted cabinets, creating the illusion of a higher ceiling.

The drama of this entrance lobby is created by walls of cleverly lit slatted dark wood that arch over a marble walkway, emphasizing the horizontal and vertical lines of the grid.

USE LIGHTING TO ENHANCE TEXTURES AND FINISHES

In this dressing room shadow-gap lighting at floor and ceiling level is combined with recessed downlights, highlighting the grooves of the wood doors and the bust by Ralph Brown.

Don't play it safe. Be adventurous with your lighting choices and experiment with different light sources and effects.

One of the intrinsic roles of accent lighting is to highlight and enhance every detail of texture – whether that's architectural lighting adding drama and definition to a space, focused spotlights targeting pieces of art or sculpture, or backlighting or undershelf lighting illuminating collections of objects. Cleverly directed beams of light, as well as indirect wall or floor washes, can draw attention to contour, shape and form, create drama with a play of light and shadow, and accentuate and enhance surface finishes and textures. Part of the design process is to experiment with different light sources and assess their effect on your chosen materials and finishes.

The lighting in this custom-made glass-fronted cabinet not only illuminates the collection of smooth and shiny objects on display, but also highlights the textural detail of the specialist plaster background chosen to contrast with them. ●----▶

STATEMENT LIGHTS

Objects of beauty in their own right and often investment pieces, statement lights add the wow factor to any space. These lights are works of art, with a sculptural quality that ensures they look almost as good unlit as when they're lit up.

Statement lights are the attention-grabbing extroverts of your lighting scheme, chosen to catch the eye and create impact and drama. They could be anything from an ornate antique chandelier to an oversized metal pendant, a floor-standing contemporary light sculpture or a cascade of hand-blown glass bubbles. Whatever the design, let it have centre stage and keep the rest of the lighting subtle so that nothing detracts from it. Here's how to create a wow factor:

● An entrance hall is a perfect place to make an impact with a statement light, as it's the first thing people see when they come in. I love an oversized pendant hung low over a round table.

● Stairwells are another favourite location. What could be more breathtaking than a tiered chandelier, spirals of sparkling crystals, or a series of lanterns cascading through several storeys? A visual treat at every level.

● Dramatic lights are magical in living and dining areas and bedrooms. Just make sure they don't block key views.

organic glass chandelier

A cascade of chain mail

Floor-to-ceiling light sculpture

oversized contemporary lantern

350 porcelain 'leaves'

Spirals of Swarovski crystals

CHOOSE SPARKLE, SHINE AND SUPERSIZE

PERSPEX RODS LIT BY CONCEALED LED LIGHTS

Metal and crystal lizard light

Mirrored-glass teardrops

Bespoke crystal chandelier

With an endless array of theatrical lighting to choose from, you can add drama and glamour to any area in the home. The only proviso is to choose a design that complements your scheme as a whole and produces the lighting effect you want.

FINISHING TOUCHES

The decorative details and accessories are what bring your home to life. These are the personal touches that reveal something of the personality and lifestyle of the inhabitants, and really make somewhere feel like 'home'. It's also the attention to design detail – the little bespoke flourishes and customizations that make something unique.

I'm a great believer in putting a personal stamp on a home. Whenever I'm designing for a client, I always strive to get into their head and to find out, not just about the colours they like and the lifestyle they lead, but also what drives them and what matters to them. The place where we live and spend so much of our time should reflect who we are and what excites us about the world – it should be the place where we can express our passions and surround ourselves with everything that brings us joy, makes us feels safe, calm and relaxed, but also inspired and energized.

OLD & NEW

Most people don't have the freedom of starting a home design completely from scratch – and for many, the idea would be a daunting prospect. The possessions we accumulate over the years tell a story about our lives, our identity, our travels, and the people and places we've loved. However ruthless we may be, to some degree or other, there will be treasured items that we want to integrate into our new home or décor. I've always found that a comfortable balance of old and new gives a space integrity and character. Whether you have heirloom pieces passed down through the family but live in a sleek city apartment, or you have a passion for modern art but live in a period property, the frisson between the two can be dynamic.

This principle also applies to the bones and fabric of your home – the architectural features such as staircases, doors, windows and fireplaces. Any building regulations permitting, updating these elements can have a dramatic impact on the feel of your home. Such changes will not only help increase a sense of space, but also provide opportunities to play with textures, materials and accent colours.

Double-width floor-to-ceiling sliding doors, with slim, long nickel handles, make a grand entrance to a kitchen.

A cocktail corner is made extra glamorous with faux-crocodile-upholstered stools, polished chrome trim on the white-lacquered bar, photography by Désirée Dolron and a vase of flowers.

DESIGNER DOORS

There is a vast scope of design possibilities for the doors in your home, which are great surfaces for introducing textural details. You may want to change their size, proportions or style for a completely new look, or decide to remove or move them to improve the interior flow.

Doors are often overlooked and given no more thought than a fresh coat of paint as part of the decorating process, but I see this as a wasted opportunity to experiment with exciting designs and materials. Think of doors as a blank canvas on which to add a new texture, tone, detail or finish. Structural changes such as enlarging openings to double width and extending the doors to the ceiling will increase the sense of volume and enhance flow. Doors can also be used to define the design grid by emphasizing the vertical and horizontal lines. The door surround itself then becomes a 'frame' for the view beyond, so don't miss the chance to create interesting vistas in both directions, with a focal point to draw the eye.

The opposite view to the one shown on page 106, looking from the kitchen into the narrow hall. When opened, the vast doors, along with the antique mirror, increase the sense of space.

DE LUXE DETAILS ELEVATE ANY DESIGN

NEW DOORS WILL ALTER THE LOOK AND FEEL OF A SPACE

Eternally elegant shoji doors are a favourite of mine, here in blackened oak with rectangular handles for a seamless finish.

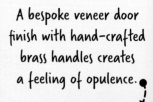

A bespoke veneer door finish with hand-crafted brass handles creates a feeling of opulence.

A large hand-cast textured nickel door pull makes a feature of an oak-veneer door. This is a great way to add a metal accent to a design scheme.

DRESS UP YOUR DOORS

A door can be designed to make a statement or to blend seamlessly with the surrounding walls. It could be single or double width, and built to open in the conventional way or to slide, pivot or concertina to save space.

Internal doors can be transparent, opaque, slatted, panelled or solid, inlaid or clad with a contrasting material or embellished with studs. Materials to consider include wood, veneer, glass, metal, leather and vellum. Wood alone presents many options, from natural grains in taupe, gold and rich brown tones, to painted, stained or lacquered.

Recessed bronze pull handles make an elegant contrast with heavily grained stained-oak doors.

Deep, dark wood panelling on the lower part of the white jib bedroom door is continued along the walls on both sides, so the door almost disappears when it's closed.

Door furniture – the handles, pulls and knobs on internal doors and built-in cupboards – presents further opportunities to make a statement by introducing contrasting textures or accent colours. Handles and pulls can also be streamlined or recessed, so they almost disappear, or designed as runners, to emphasize the vertical or horizontal grid lines. I often think of door furniture as another decorative accessory – the jewellery of the room – and might choose anything from crystal, leather or horn to hammered, blackened or shiny polished metal, to complement the rest of the scheme.

PLAY AROUND WITH DIFFERENT FINISHES AND TEXTURES

MIRRORS

Whether they're hung singly, in pairs or in groups, mirrors are a magical way to embellish the home with another layer of decoration and texture. With endless sizes, shapes and finishes to choose from, there are designs to suit any interior.

Mirrors work on so many levels. First and foremost is the practical function, especially in dressing rooms, bathrooms and hallways, where they ensure you can put outfits together with confidence, carry out essential grooming rituals and check your appearance before leaving the house.

Mirrors also create wonderful effects through their ability to reflect light and 'bounce' it around a room. Strategically placed opposite a window, a mirror will amplify the levels of natural light coming into a space and make it seem lighter and brighter. This is also true of artificial light, and enchanting effects can be achieved when mirrors are positioned to reflect decorative lights, such as chandeliers, strands of sparkling crystals or clusters of glass bubbles. The way mirrors reflect light around a space has a dynamic, energizing effect.

This ornamental mirror adds organic curves and a gold accent to the neutral décor.

This ornate mirror with its carved gold frame is one of a pair in a hallway, reflecting a view of the living and dining area opposite.

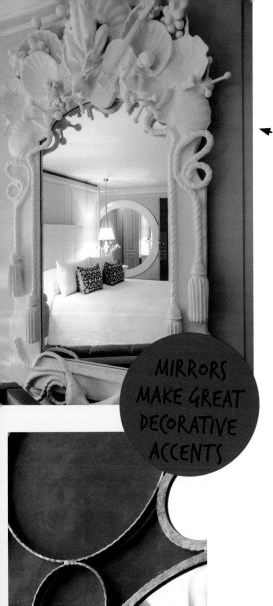

A whimsical Objet Trouvé mirror, designed by Codor, brings a wonderful sense of intrigue to this soothing pale neutral bedroom scheme.

MIRRORS MAKE GREAT DECORATIVE ACCENTS

This sculptural design made up of gold-leaf circles is a mirror-cum-artwork.

Mirrors can also be used to create the illusion of a space being larger than it actually is. Creating a reflected image of a small room makes it feel more expansive, while reflections of adjoining spaces through open doorways, or of rooms leading off narrow corridors or hallways, also help to improve the sense of flow through an interior.

Finally, mirrors are decorative objects in their own right, adding a finishing touch to any style of décor. You can choose antique or contemporary designs, with frames that are ornately carved and opulent or simply formed and rustic. They can be large or small in size, and rectangular, circular or irregular in shape, with a finish that is rough or smooth, shiny or matt, and understated or glamorous.

" Mirrors can be enjoyed on many levels — for their light-reflecting, space-enhancing qualities, and for their aesthetic appeal. "

MAKE A STATEMENT

Mirrors offer a wonderful opportunity to create a feature or make a dramatic impact. I might achieve this by playing with proportion and scale – such as hanging an oversized mirror in a small space – or through textural contrast – for instance, juxtaposing a shiny lacquer or glamorous gold-leaf finish with a textured plaster wall.

Another way I create drama with mirrors is by how I arrange them. Mirrors can be hung on walls, of course, but they can also be placed on the floor, or on a shelf or ledge, depending on size, and propped up against a wall. Repetition of shape or line is always effective, so I often use pairs of mirrors in halls or on either side of a door, or hang them in groups. Many designs resemble works of art or sculpture in their own right, but even more so when they're arranged in an unusual configuration to create a form of dynamic art installation.

ORGANIC SHAPES

Mirrors are a brilliant way to introduce circles, curves and irregular organic shapes into a design scheme, providing an instant foil to balance out the architectural lines and straight edges elsewhere in the room. It's not just about the shape of the mirror – which may be repeated or opposed by other elements in the room – but also the composition that it reflects. The shapes in the 'picture' framed by the mirror will either echo or contrast with it.

The glossy taupe-lacquered mirror frame is part of the textural story in this tonal bedroom, with its rich mix of linens, crushed silk velvets, silk carpet, leather and specialist plaster. Its circular shape acts as a foil for all the straight lines.

This supersized circular mirror captures the light from the window opposite and maximizes its effect, while the reflection of the classic ball chair is echoed by the mirror's dark circular frame.

This series of deep-rimmed circular mirrors is reminiscent of dividing cells.

A large convex mirror, one of a pair on either side of a bedroom door, bounces light around an upstairs corridor and creates almost abstract reflections. The curved seat of the vintage stool beneath it echoes the circular shape.

An irregular group of iron-framed mirrors reflect the bedroom opposite.

BANNERS & RUNNERS

For me, banners and runners are essential components of any successful design scheme. They can be interpreted in so many different ways and expressed in such a variety of materials and finishes that the creative possibilities are off the chart.

NUMBER ONE IN MY DESIGN ARSENAL

One of my ultimate design signatures, banners and runners are, in a nutshell, sections of one material that have usually been inset or inlaid into, or sometimes applied to or laid over, another contrasting material. They may be wide or narrow, vertical or horizontal, and can be used on everything from floors and walls to furniture and soft furnishings.

MULTIFUNCTIONAL

Banners and runners are the hard-working, multitasking heroes of a design, as they have several roles to play. Foremost among these is the fundamental part they play in reinforcing the design grid (see page 22).

As you may remember, the grid is my way of dividing up a space three-dimensionally so that I can see how to structure its design. Through the grid system I can alter any proportions and correct a room's symmetry, which in turn helps to increase the sense of space and volume, and makes the room feel more balanced. The grid structure also allows me to determine the optimum layout and zoning for a room, together with its furniture,

fittings and lighting, and thus achieve a comfortable sense of flow throughout the space.

Banners and runners are used to emphasize the vertical and horizontal lines of the grid, helping to create balance. Defining the horizontals will make a room feel longer or wider, while highlighting the verticals will give the illusion that the walls and ceiling are taller than they are.

Runners are also used to draw the eye through a space – either to call attention to a focal point or to help you navigate your way through the space with ease. Floor runners, in particular, can be designed to form a kind of walkway through an interior, leading you along a corridor or towards a door, staircase or seating area, for example. They may also be continued up walls or even onto ceilings. In this way, runners can help to connect spaces together, forming links between adjoining zones or rooms and creating a sense of unity. These connections can also be reinforced visually by repeating a material texture, or an accent colour or finish that has been used elsewhere in a different way or in different proportions. This has the effect of a design echo, promoting a feeling of harmony through the home as a whole.

This eclectic double-height living space plays with scale, with the dramatic black marble runner making a feature of the fireplace wall and drawing the eye to the Gavin Turk artwork alongside it. The grid is further defined by the floor-to-ceiling curtains.

AESTHETICS

Runners and banners may also be introduced into a design scheme for their aesthetic value – and for the endless opportunities they provide for setting up unusual and arresting juxtapositions of tones and textures. One of the joys of using banners and runners is that they allow you to bring in relatively small quantities of an expensive material or finish that you love, but that would otherwise overshoot the budget. This touch of luxe can be just what's needed to elevate your design into something truly special. A banner of specialist plaster on one wall will become a focal point, while narrow slivers of polished metal, mother-of-pearl, leather or marble will add instant glamour and a feeling of luxury.

In terms of suitable materials, almost anything goes, as long as it works with the rest of your decorating scheme. You can pair hard with hard, soft with

The inlaid brass band on these imposing dark timber doors incorporates the door handle for a streamlined effect. This detail reflects the narrow dark marble runner set into the marble floor.

The vast structural columns in a former auction house clad with pale taupe wood panels, inset with horizontal runners of polished brass and nickel.

soft, or mix the two; and you can use contrasting colours or similar tones in opposing textures. The crucial thing is to have runners installed professionally, as anything less than perfectly executed joins will spoil the effect. Here are just a few of my favourite banner and runner ideas:

● Walls: textured black plaster above a fireplace with white walls; coloured glass through rough plaster; dark wood cutting through rough natural stone; tone-on-tone taupe polished plaster against matt taupe walls.

● Floors: polished stainless-steel through gold-toned wood; white resin or marble through black oak; narrow brass through dark wood or marble.

● Joinery: room divider of horizontal slats of dark wood; cupboard doors of vertical slats of taupe wood; polished nickel strip on a taupe wood door; shiny brass strip on a lacquered table.

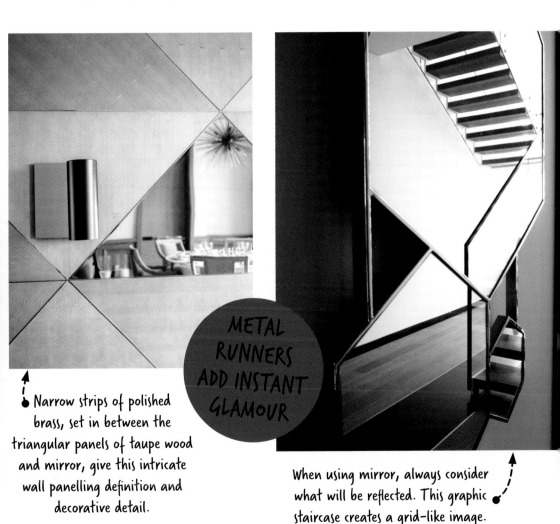

METAL RUNNERS ADD INSTANT GLAMOUR

● Narrow strips of polished brass, set in between the triangular panels of taupe wood and mirror, give this intricate wall panelling definition and decorative detail.

When using mirror, always consider what will be reflected. This graphic staircase creates a grid-like image.

DECORATIVE DISPLAYS

How you choose to accessorize your home is an important part of the design process and shouldn't be an afterthought. This is your moment to showcase the things you love and give your interior that all-important personal touch.

Decorating or redesigning your home provides the perfect opportunity to reassess your possessions and look at them with fresh eyes. Objects and art that you know you love should be considered early on in the design process, so you know exactly where and how these pieces will be displayed – the furniture or objects that will be around them, how they will be lit and what their backdrop will be. This ensures shelves will be fixed at exactly the right height and niches will be built to the correct dimensions.

On a floating shelf, painted the same colour as the wall so it blends into the background, a row of evenly spaced simple glass vases enclose single stems of white roses.

You may want to treat certain treasured items or collections as star pieces and select the other elements of your design scheme especially to work with them. On the other hand, if you have objects or pictures that

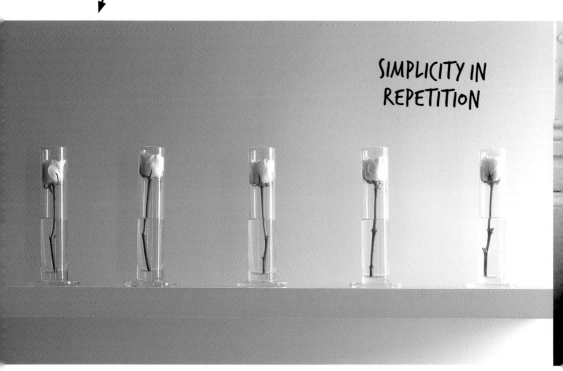

SIMPLICITY IN REPETITION

really don't seem to fit in with your new scheme, ask yourself whether it's time they were passed on to a new home. Any items that you can't bear to part with can always be boxed up and put into storage, to be rediscovered anew at some future date.

ALL THAT YOU LOVE

I'm no minimalist and in my own home I love to display sculpture and art – especially black-and-white photographs, which seem to hold a certain old-school glamour and always look stylish in any setting. I tend to hang large pictures on the wall – always at the right height to be gazed at levelly, without craning your neck – but smaller ones are often propped up along shelves. This appeals to me as a more relaxed way to display, as you can easily move things around if the mood takes you.

I also have crystals, Buddhas, resin coral and always plenty of fresh flowers. These all inspire me and keep my home flowing with positive energy.

A pair of smooth marble globes on the slate hearth of a fireplace contrast with the lines of the traditional carved marble fire surround and the charred bricks.

Resin coral is one of my favourite ways to introduce organic shapes and texture to a room. Here the delicacy of the branches stands out against the solid wood surface.

TEXTURAL CONTRAST ON A SMALL SCALE

GROUPING OBJECTS WITH A COMMON THEME ALWAYS CREATES IMPACT

Tall glass vases, with an arum lily in each, break up a row of anthropology domes encasing textural resin coral.

HOW TO DISPLAY

The first thing to look at is what you are going to display and then think about the best way to showcase it. This means not only making choices about where in the room, and on or in what, but also deciding on the materials, textures, colours and lighting that will set off your collections to best effect.

If it's art, for example, assess the dominant colours and textures within the work or works, and plan your wall colours and finishes to complement them. Think about what else will be around the display wall, and from where the art will mostly be viewed.

Whether it's a piece of sculpture, a stash of books, a collection of porcelain or an eclectic group of treasures that you're going to display, think about whether you want them on shelves, in display cabinets, on a mantelpiece or on a tabletop. If you like the idea of shelves, what do you have in mind? A single low-level shelf running the length of the room? Or a wall of cubbyholes of different sizes to accommodate various items, including books and maybe even your TV and media equipment? Are the shelves chunky, minimal, floating, or built into an alcove or around a doorframe to make the most of 'dead' space? If you'd like a display cabinet, will it be a built-in unit or a free-standing dresser? Will it have an open front or enclose the contents behind glass?

A display of vases and black-and-white photography is offset by a backdrop of Calacatta marble in this glamorous entrance hall.

The symmetry of this composition is broken up by varying the objects' heights, textures and tones.

"

Don't try to include too much in one display, and leave breathing space around objects — sometimes less is more.

"

Designing a study using a stylish combination of taupe tones and dark chocolate timber with accents of red creates impact and surprise.

oversized rotund planters of box topiary create drama through a play of scale alongside the smaller accessories.

Three white ceramic vases of greenery, placed in a row, impose a sense of order and harmony.

A curved sculpture stands out against the marble counter inlaid with brass.

Lit from above, a marble Buddha floats on a Perspex perch in a marble niche.

Three is the magic number and creates a 'wow' with the simplest of objects, like these vibrant arum lilies in glass fishbowls.

CREATING A COMPOSITION

I find that often the most effective way to display objects is to group like with like. Even the most inexpensive and simple collection of white ceramics or glass vases, for example, will have an impact when they are gathered together on a shelf or tabletop, or in a niche or display cabinet.

Depending on the nature of the collection, you can either align identical items in uniform rows, or create a more fluid and relaxed composition. The latter is a good solution for items that are not identical but have a common theme. For instance, an evenly spaced line of identical white bowls makes a visual statement through simple repetition, while a group of glass vases of varying shapes and sizes can be arranged in an asymmetrical but balanced way, with taller items positioned towards the back.

When you're creating a tableau or vignette with a group of objects, it's easiest to start in the centre and work outwards, playing around with the heights and shapes, taking things out and moving things around until you achieve the effect you like.

CREATE IMPACT WITH A LINE OR ROWS OF IDENTICAL OBJECTS

MOOD-BOOSTING DISPLAYS

The Arts and Crafts designer William Morris advised that you should only have items in your home that you know to be beautiful or believe to be useful. It's a good principle to bear in mind when you're assessing your possessions and creating displays. I'm a great believer that you should have on show the items that you use regularly and that give you pleasure to look at. Anything that doesn't inspire you or bring you joy – or that you wouldn't want visitors to see – should be kept behind closed doors.

I'm very conscious of the energy in an interior, as it needs to be free-flowing for the space to feel harmonious and uplifting. The ancient philosophy of Feng shui lies at the heart of this and is something I always consider when I'm designing the grid and layout. Promoting good energy is also why I include organic pieces. Flowers, foliage and other natural elements are a key part of this, adding further layers of colour, texture and scent. The size and form of floral displays should be tailored to the setting where they'll be displayed – an elaborate arrangement in a hallway, for instance, a line of single stems in identical containers along a shelf, or a bowl of succulents on a coffee table. I generally keep displays to one or two toning colours, plus green, and will often echo an accent colour used elsewhere in the room.

One star piece can be all you need to make a statement, such as this stunning vintage copper snail sculpture by Robert Kuo, which takes pride of place on a roof terrace.

Patterned glass vases of varying heights display pompom flowers on a marble and metal console.

THEME DISPLAYS BY TONE OR TEXTURE

" You don't have to spend a fortune to create eye-catching displays — everyday items can look stunning in the right context. **"**

A dressing room is the ultimate luxury and I've given mine a touch of Hollywood glamour with black-and-white photography, fresh flowers and open storage.

3

Room by Room

Here's where you pull all the elements together to let your ideas crystallize and make your dream home a reality.

Now is the time to put
those design principles into
action to create the home
you want to live in. Drawing
all the different components
together, you now have the
tools to tailor each room in your
home to suit your practical needs,
your way of life and your personal
style. Every room in the home has
a unique set of requirements and
considerations, and the following
pages will help you to approach each
space with confidence. Decorating a
home, especially if it involves a major
redesign, can be a daunting prospect,
but if you have planned it well, and have
researched your suppliers and workforce
carefully, it can also be extremely rewarding.
There is nothing more exciting than seeing your
ideas starting to take shape.

FIRST
IMPRESSIONS
ARE IMPORTANT
SO MAKE YOURS
COUNT

ENTRANCES, HALLWAYS & CIRCULATION SPACES

Connecting areas are often overlooked or treated as an afterthought, but in fact they are a crucial part of your home. Collectively, they link all the rooms together, so their design can help to set the tone for your home as a whole.

Halls, corridors, landings and staircases are like the bone structure of a home, quietly playing a supporting role to the more extrovert rooms that wow us with their personality and style. However, these spaces shouldn't be neglected in the design stakes. Although they are not usually somewhere to linger, they are passed through frequently and this should be a pleasant experience. It is also a good reason for making an impact, as you may feel emboldened to experiment with more adventurous colour, dramatic texture or graphic pattern when you will be experiencing it in relatively small doses.

FIRST IMPRESSIONS

The front door and entrance hall are the first things people see when they come to your home, and they set the tone for what is to come. As you step through the doorway – as either a guest or a resident – you want to feel as though you are being welcomed into a warm, comfortable sanctuary, where any worries or stresses instantly melt away.

Putting a personal stamp on your front door is a great way to make a home your own, whether that's rejuvenating an existing door with a bold colour or finish – such as inlay or studs – and dramatic, oversized door furniture, or replacing it with a new design. I love to upscale a front door as it's an instant way to make a real statement.

The entrance of my London home is bold, graphic and glamorous, with the design grid much in evidence through the black-and-white marble floor, pivoting lacquered shutters, panel of specialist plaster, tall double doors and trio of pendant lights.

DESIGN & DÉCOR

Designing the main entrance hall is not only about creating a good first impression, however. It's also significant because this core space is likely to be glimpsed from within all the key living areas that lead off it. Think of every doorway in your home as a frame for a view, and make sure the vista seen from both directions is a pleasing one.

In the entrance hall itself, remember that the front door will be a prominent feature and so must look as good from the inside as it does from the outside, while also imbuing the interior with a sense of safety and security. Look at ways to make a dramatic style statement here, by creating a focal point to catch the eye as soon as you enter, engaging your attention and drawing you in. This could be a luxurious wall finish, a theatrical piece of lighting or an arresting artwork.

Use the grid system to help you design the space, and consider creating runners of contrasting materials on the floors or walls to lead you onwards (see pages 86–9 and 116–19). On a practical level, it's also essential to build in sufficient storage for items such as coats, umbrellas, shopping bags and shoes.

When you are choosing the décor for your hallway and connecting areas, aim to create a sympathetic relationship between them and the rooms leading directly off them. There needs to be a design thread or common theme to link these spaces together, so that nothing jars. You might choose to treat these areas as an extension of the primary living rooms, resulting in a calm, coherent feel, with one space flowing seamlessly into another. Alternatively, you could take a bolder approach and give connecting areas their own design identity. An echo of a colour, or a repeated texture or material used in the room beyond is all that is needed to create a sense of unity. A good tip is to lay the design board you create for the hallway next to those for the adjoining rooms. That way, you can ensure that the same design dialogue is being spoken and that everything sits together comfortably.

As well as exuding warmth and hospitality, a hallway should generate a sense of excitement and expectation about what lies beyond.

EVERY DOORWAY
FRAMES A VIEW

CONNECT & UNIFY, CREATE LINKS & IMPACT

A sense of anticipation is created by the dramatic double doors that open onto a black wood runner set into polished stone, guiding the eye to the statement pieces beyond.

CORRIDORS

Give the connecting areas in your home the same design consideration as any other space. In particular, think about the flow of colour, texture and materials through the home as a whole and ensure there is a sense of continuity.

GOOD LIGHTING MAKES CORRIDORS FEEL WARM AND INVITING

The skirting board in this hallway was replaced with a light baffle, bathing the dark wood floor in a warm glow. Ceiling spots highlight the Peter Beard artwork and the Christian Liaigre banquettes.

A series of dark oak doorframes along the length of this monochrome corridor defines the grid and draws the eye.

Corridors and hallways often don't benefit from much natural light, so it's important to get the artificial lighting right, both for practical reasons and to ensure the space feels inviting. Reflective surfaces also help to enhance lighting effects. Low-level lighting that bathes the floor in light and bounces it off the walls is one of my favourite solutions. If the ceiling is high enough, a series of pendants will draw the eye along the space, while recessed downlights are also an option.

Shiny surfaces, including waxed-plaster walls, a marble floor runner that continues from the entrance hall, glass and accents of brass reflect and maximize natural light.

White walls, displaying a collection of black-and-white photography, taupe oak flooring and lighting that washes both surfaces in warm light create a calm connecting area.

Like mini galleries, corridors can be great places to hang art or display a star piece.

STAIRS

Running through the very core of the home, the staircase is a prominent architectural feature that not only plays a structural role, but also a stylistic one. Changing the design of the staircase can completely transform the proportions and feel of a space.

Staircases are feats of engineering and replacing them is expensive, complex and disruptive. However, if you have the budget to employ an architect to conceptualize your stairway to heaven, and the specialists to actualize it to a high standard, you won't regret it. Whether you like the idea of a graceful sweeping curve, an imposing dramatic statement or an open-tread design that appears to be floating, a bespoke staircase can be like a functional sculpture, winding its way through the very heart of your home.

This glamorous staircase was one of the first elements I designed for the apartment, and the impressive structure became one of its key stylistic features.

THE STAIRS ARE THE BACKBONE OF A HOME

STAIRCASE STYLE

If you're not able to undertake a redesign – due to either budgetary or planning restrictions – there are many ways to revamp an existing staircase so it's in keeping with the rest of your home. The banisters can be boxed in or replaced, and the handrail exchanged for a bespoke design in a material of your choice. The walls can be clad, panelled or given a specialist textured finish. The treads and risers can also be clad, if deep enough, or painted or carpeted with a runner – I love a silk carpet edged with leather.

Good lighting is also key and must be controllable from every level. Shadow-gap lighting creates a sleek effect and makes the stairs glow, while low-level recessed lights bathe the treads with pools of light. A dramatic chandelier or pendant cascading through the stairwell will add a sense of excitement.

Made of lustrous black metal and taupe wood, which tones with the specialist plaster on the walls, this sinuous staircase pours through two storeys, with the same materials continued along a mezzanine to link the areas together.

REDESIGNING THE STAIRCASE ALTERS THE FEEL OF THE WHOLE SPACE

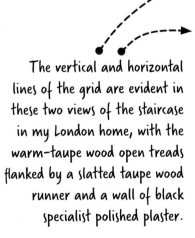

The vertical and horizontal lines of the grid are evident in these two views of the staircase in my London home, with the warm-taupe wood open treads flanked by a slatted taupe wood runner and a wall of black specialist polished plaster.

KITCHENS & DINING SPACES

So much more than just a place to prepare, cook and eat food, the kitchen in most modern homes is a central hub of activity. Essentially, it's the headquarters of the home – not only a place to deal with household admin, but also increasingly somewhere to make business calls, join online meetings, complete school work or home crafts and just hang out.

The kitchen is invariably where we spend a great deal of our time when we're at home, either alone or with other members of the household. People tend to gravitate towards the kitchen, and it's often the first room we head for when we come home. We expect so much from this space – in terms of all the different activities we want to be able to carry out there, as well as the practical functions we need it to fulfil – that getting the design right has never been more important.

Added to which, there is no getting away from the fact that kitchens are expensive – from the units and appliances to the lighting, furniture and gadgets. Installing a new kitchen from scratch is a significant financial outlay, so it pays not to make mistakes. Thorough research, planning and preparation from the outset really is time well spent. I often equate kitchen design with a complicated jigsaw puzzle where precision is everything. One size most definitely doesn't fit all, so it can prove invaluable to enlist the skills of a professional kitchen designer to help you achieve the result that works well for you and the way you live.

The strong linear elements that emphasize the grid in this monochrome kitchen are balanced out by the organic shapes and soft curves, while the wonderful mix of textures and finishes gives the space its character.

At one end of an open-plan space, this kitchen was designed to echo the décor used elsewhere.

The in-line hob is set into a stainless-steel counter that runs at right angles to the main worktop, with a breakfast bar on the other side.

Whether you choose to have a separate dining room or zone off a portion of your kitchen to create an eating area is a matter of personal preference. Of course, it also depends on how much space you have available in your home – these days, a dedicated dining room is often sacrificed in place of a TV room, playroom or home office.

DINING ROOMS

If you love entertaining and regularly hold dinner parties, a more formal dining room that's entirely separate from the kitchen where you prepare food and cook meals may be a priority for you. But do think carefully about where you site a dedicated dining room, as it needs to be within easy reach of the kitchen so that you don't spend all evening traipsing up and down stairs or along corridors with dishes of food that are getting cold.

This is a room that will mainly be used in the evenings and for long weekend lunches, so you can really go to town with the decoration and use sumptuous materials, dramatic colours or bold pattern to create something extraordinary. Glamorous finishes, such as shiny lacquer, polished plaster, marble, mirror, gold leaf, crystal and silverware, will all reflect the light and give the room a feeling of opulence. They'll also look magical by candlelight and contribute to the overall ambience that you'll want to create so your guests feel that they've had an exceptional experience.

A curved bench on one side of the round table gives this eating or study area in the corner of a kitchen a sense of seclusion.

This dining area is defined by a change of flooring, with the furniture placed on an area of taupe marble set into the dark wood floor. The same wood is then repeated on the wall behind, in the form of a backlit floating panel that gives the space presence.

The table and chairs are the star pieces in a dining space and will set the style for the rest of the furniture and furnishings. Round tables are conducive for intimate gatherings, while rectangular tables work well for larger parties and make it easy to work with the grid. Don't just buy the largest table that will fit in the space. If you won't be seating twelve for dinner on a regular basis, those empty chairs will dampen the vibe. If you want your guests to relax and linger a while, choose chairs that are comfortable and supportive.

The graceful curves of Hans Wegner's classic Wishbone chairs balance out the hard lines of this solid wood dining table.

In this simply furnished dining room, the white-painted trestle table echoes the fabric runners on the walls. These were made from white calico and sewn onto sand fabric, which was stapled onto wooden battens to cover the walls.

CIRCLES AND CURVES
OFFSET HARD LINES

Two views of the kitchen on page 139, with the dining space (above) given a sense of separation from the working area (right) by the drawer unit displaying a row of rosemary plants. The dark wood table and white leather chairs from Modénature tie in with the monochrome scheme.

EATING AREAS

If you don't have a suitable room for a dedicated dining room, or if your lifestyle doesn't call for one, a comfortable eating area within a kitchen can be just as inviting and stylish. If you're a confident cook who doesn't get flustered by the presence of an audience, this type of setup also allows you to chat with your guests while you prepare the food. For many, the ultimate luxury is to have both an area within the kitchen for casual meals and a formal dining room for special occasions.

In a typical narrow town house, an all-encompassing open-plan design, where an entire floor is dedicated to a large, inclusive kitchen with a working area and breakfast bar at one end, and a dining area at the other, can be a very successful solution. Such designs benefit from natural light entering the space from the front and back, where perhaps floor-to-ceiling glass opens onto a garden or terrace. The absence of dividing walls also increases natural light and ensures one area flows easily into another.

A group of textural vases elevates a bowl of eggs into a decorative display.

LAYOUTS

Major factors in determining how successful and practical such a space proves to be are the layout and décor. As always, there should be a natural sense of flow throughout, which can be achieved by designing on the grid (see page 22). The layout should be ergonomic and practical, so you're not running laps around the table or island, knocking your hip on the sharp corner of a worktop or zigzagging uncomfortably around furniture.

In the working area of a kitchen, you need to ensure that movement between the sink, fridge, hob and oven is seamless, with plenty of space on the worktop near the sink and oven to chop vegetables and put hot dishes down. In a dining area, the crucial thing is to allow sufficient clear space around the table and chairs so you can still walk around it when people are seated.

In terms of the décor, while each distinct area needs to have its own personality, the overall space should have a unified feel. The easiest way to achieve this is to stick to the same colour scheme while repeating materials throughout, and to introduce runners of contrasting flooring to lead the way from one zone to the next.

A MIX OF MATT AND SHINY SURFACES ADDS GLAMOUR

A dining room at the front of the house leads into a kitchen, which in turn flows into a conservatory and garden beyond. The space is unified by the monochrome palette with accents of pink, purple and bronze. Black wood, poured resin and granite play against white walls, glossy cabinets and leather chairs.

> **❝** Kitchen design is highly personal, so spend time thinking about your priorities and plan yours accordingly. **❞**

YOUR DESIGN BRIEF

When you're embarking on a new kitchen, now is the time to consider whether the existing location is the best one for how you live. I often see kitchens in basement conversions, which means they're often largely reliant on artificial light, even during daylight hours. While the idea of rerouting utilities can seem daunting and does come at an extra cost, the result can be well worth it.

Whether you decide to relocate the kitchen or reconfigure the existing one, careful planning is the key to success. Ideally, enlist a kitchen designer to help you, but at the very least visit as many showrooms as possible, take precise measurements and be very clear about what you want. Here are some questions to get you thinking:

- What sort of dining area do you want in your kitchen – a table and chairs to seat eight, an intimate space for four or just a breakfast bar?

- What other activities will be carried out here on a regular basis, such as crafts or homework?

- Can you accommodate a separate utility room or area for pets?

- Are you a keen cook or do you avoid cooking as much as possible? If you are, what sort of food do you like to make and does this require any specialist equipment?

- Do you want an audiovisual system or air-conditioning?

ART AND STAR PIECES LOOK GREAT IN A DINING AREA

Once you have honed your wish list and established what is practical and possible within the constraints of your available space and budget, you can start to build and refine your design board. Try to shop around – not just for the best deals, but also because the end result will be more interesting and characterful if you mix and match furniture and accessories, rather than buying it all from one supplier.

SURFACES & MATERIALS

There is a vast choice of materials and finishes that can be used to stunning effect in kitchens – for walls and floor, cabinets, worktops and splashbacks. Wood, glass, stone, ceramic, stainless steel, lacquer and concrete are just some of the options – not to mention any number of composites that are often very durable as well as stylish. Each has its own aesthetic and practical attributes, so do your research. There's no point installing an

expensive sink that stains easily, a floor that shows up every scuff or a worktop that requires more maintenance than you have time for. Make sure the materials you choose are fit for purpose as well as pleasing to look at.

FURNITURE & APPLIANCES

Your choice of appliances will probably be determined by your cooking skills. It's all too easy to be seduced into buying the latest must-have gadget, but if you never use it, that state-of-the-art bread-maker just becomes another item to store. Be realistic about your requirements – I don't cook much, but I would never be without a tap that provides instant boiling water. Taps are like pieces of sculpture, so it's worth splashing out on one that is the designer piece of your kitchen.

When you're choosing furniture, comfort is paramount. Always test seating before you buy and ensure it's the right height for your table or breakfast bar. I love a mix of chairs and benches, and often play with scale by placing an oversized carver at each end of a rectangular table.

In one corner of the working end of my kitchen is this informal eating area, with built-in banquettes around a taupe lacquer table and backlit shelves behind.

The kitchen itself (right) is separated from the main dining area (below) by the Carrara marble breakfast bar, which echoes the lines of the table and the bronze light that hangs above it. Every element in this vast space emphasizes the grid.

KITCHEN LIGHTING

A kitchen needs to look warm and inviting at all times, with plenty of practical task lighting where you need it, as well as versatile atmospheric and statement lighting to suit the different activities you will be undertaking here.

Successful kitchen lighting relies on building up layers of task, background and decorative lighting, which can be used in different combinations according to your requirements. If the kitchen incorporates several different zones, this is even more important, as lighting can be used to help define these areas and allows you to make some spaces brighter than others, as appropriate. The more circuits there are, the more options you have for adjusting the lighting to suit your needs, while dimmers offer even more versatility. This enables you to set levels of light to suit various activities and moods.

The long table in my main dining area aligns precisely with the runner of black specialist plaster, while the structural beam and columns, clad in taupe wood and trimmed with brass, frame the composition. Ceiling spots and uplights bring out the textures of the materials and reflect off the shiny surfaces.

DON'T FORGET TO HIGHLIGHT TEXTURAL SURFACES

TYPES OF LIGHT FOR KITCHENS

Targeted spotlights are ideal for task lighting, as you can direct the beams where you need them, including onto surfaces to highlight textures. A line of pendants over an island or table is also an attractive option. Low-level lighting under units makes them appear to float, while lighting above them creates a soft glow on the wall and ceiling. Lights can be recessed under cabinets to light the worktops, and shelves and display units can be backlit.

I designed the magnificent linear bronze light suspended over my dining table. It emphasizes the horizontal lines of the grid and is reminiscent of structural beams in an echo of the vertical support columns in this former auction house.

LIGHTING CAN ALTER THE MOOD OF A SPACE IN AN INSTANT

DINING SPACE LIGHTING

Lighting is an instant way to alter the mood of a space and really comes into its own where eating areas are concerned. Within an inclusive kitchen, the lighting over the table and breakfast bar should be dimmable, so you can lower it to create a conducive atmospheric for eating in the evening, but brighten it when the space is being used for admin or homework.

Directional ceiling spotlights work well over a breakfast bar, especially if the ceiling is low, while a series of pendants is a more decorative option. Architectural lighting under its base creates an attractive effect and bathes the floor in a soft, atmospheric glow.

LIGHTING THE TABLE

The choice of lighting for your dining table will largely depend on its shape and size, as well as the style of the space as a whole. I'm a firm believer in making a statement here, as this is a great way to give presence to a dining zone and imbue it with its own identity. If you have a long rectangular table, a line of pendants, either at the same or staggered heights, is a good option. You could also choose a linear design, with a similar effect to the one I designed for my home (see page 149). A cluster

This dining area is enclosed in a 'cage' of narrow wood beams, making it feel cosy yet still open. Tom Dixon's nickel-plated aluminium Gem pendants add a sense of opulence and reflect light off their faceted surfaces.

of lights is effective over a square table, while a theatrical chandelier or single oversize pendant suspended centrally over a round table is one of my favourite ways to create impact with playful contrasts of scale. Make sure lighting is hung at the correct height so as not to obstruct views across the tabletop. Always think about the colour, texture and finish of your lighting, too, and make sure it works as part of your overall scheme. Finally, remember to include candles, which never fail to create a flattering glow.

This dining space is given presence in a minimal kitchen by the vast Avico light by Fontana Arte, hanging directly over a circular black wood table surrounded by tub chairs covered in pale glazed linen. The gentle contours and organic, petal-like configuration is emphasized by the backdrop of the built-in cupboards.

OVERSIZED LIGHTS ADD AN INSTANT TWIST

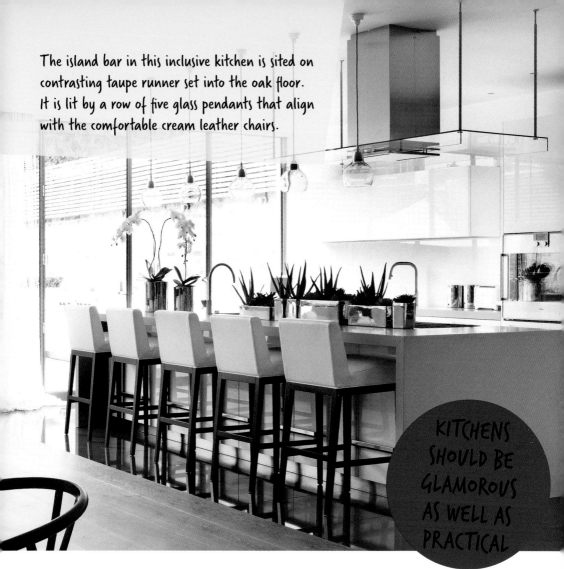

The island bar in this inclusive kitchen is sited on contrasting taupe runner set into the oak floor. It is lit by a row of five glass pendants that align with the comfortable cream leather chairs.

KITCHENS SHOULD BE GLAMOROUS AS WELL AS PRACTICAL

KELLY'S KITCHEN KEYNOTES

There is so much choice available – for everything from kitchen units, fittings and appliances to surfaces, furniture, lighting and accessories – that it can be hard to know where to start. Below is a checklist of a few of my favourite ideas or must-haves for kitchens:

• A rich textural mix, especially shiny with matt: wood with lacquer, glass with stone, leather with chrome or nickel.

• Multiple layers of dimmable lighting on individual circuits.

• A dramatic pendant over a table in an unusual material or super-sized scale.

• Units in textured wood or shiny lacquer, with customized drawer space and open displays.

• A breakfast bar at a counter or an island with comfortable bar chairs.

The main dining area in this house is simple yet super-glamorous. The focal point of the room is the nickel-framed fireplace set high in the wall like art. The sleek marble table with cream leather and nickel chairs is lit from above by a row of cylindrical glass pendants.

MARBLE ALWAYS LOOKS LUXURIOUS

• Low-level lighting that washes the floor and makes units appear to float.

• Reflective surfaces that play with light and add a sense of glamour.

• Classic combinations such as wood, marble and glass – always so stylish.

• Details such as taps and door furniture that elevate your design.

The furniture, lighting and taps are pieces of sculpture for your kitchen, so choose them to make an impact.

LIVING ROOMS

Today's living rooms are just that in every sense – rooms for living in. They're where we chill after work, watch TV and read, enjoy time with family and friends – chatting, laughing and partying. As with kitchens, they've become spaces that we expect to be versatile – formal enough to entertain in, but also comfortable and welcoming, inviting us to kick back and relax.

How and when you intend to use your living room – and consequently how you decide to design and decorate it – will depend in part on the size of your home and how much available space you have to play with. Generally, a formal living room that's reserved for 'best' is a thing of the past. Today's preference for open-plan living means that frequently the living area occupies one zone in an all-encompassing space – an expansive kitchen with a seating area at one end, or a living room that includes a dining table and chairs or a home office are all popular solutions.

The first task is to assess your space and, being realistic, decide what you want from it. Will it be a standalone room, partially separated or one area within a fully open-plan space? The latter is what I have in my current home (see right and overleaf). When is the living area going to be used and by whom? If you will be sharing it with young children, teenagers or pets, this

will probably have a bearing on your choice of furniture and furnishings. Finally, think about the activities that will be carried out here and what that involves. Would you like a quiet corner for reading and shelves for all your books? A TV and media equipment – or is there room for a separate den?

ALWAYS BALANCE HARD LINES WITH CURVES

This console table and pair of armchairs act as a space divider between zones.

The open-plan ground floor of my home is split into three main areas — kitchen at the back, dining space in the middle and living area at the front.

I made a feature of the original structural columns by cladding them in taupe wood trimmed with brass. They emphasize the grid and frame views through the space while contributing to the textural and tonal story.

The linear sofa, with the long marble shelf opposite, define the perimeters of the space, while the angular coffee table and armchairs break up the symmetry and create balance. The giant glass lights add impact without blocking views.

When I'm designing an interior, I like to spend time in the space so I can really get a feel for it and understand how to work with it. I start to visualize the lines of the grid in three dimensions and this informs how I begin to plan the layout. I decide what structural changes need to be made, if any, and think about how to incorporate original features, such as the vast supporting columns in my home, a former auction house. Period details can be given a new lease of life by juxtaposing them with contemporary designs and sleek finishes.

WHERE TO BEGIN

Creating a design board for the living room will help your ideas take shape, and I always start the process by laying down lots of fabric samples in textures and tones that I like. I avoid thinking about what I'll use each of them for and just begin to build up a tonal palette that will set the mood. Make the design board as detailed as possible – include every element, down to the last detail – and don't rush it. Leave it in the room so you can refer to it and tweak it if necessary. Consider the elements in the following order:

Fabrics Create the tonal/textural palette.
Furniture Look at form and texture.
Details Introduce contrast – door panels, trims, inlays, cushion buttons and bands.
Star pieces Art, collections, furniture.
Window treatments Shutters, blinds, sheer curtains or heavy drapes.
Floors and walls These must complement the rest of the scheme, not compete with it.
Lighting Plan this key component once the other design decisions have been made.

In an open-plan design, give each zone a distinct personality but keep the overall palette harmonious and unified.

CREATING ZONES

In most homes the living room is a multipurpose space that's required to accommodate a range of activities and fulfil various roles – as both a private sanctuary where the householder can unwind and a public space that is welcoming for visitors.

Whether your living area is sited within a large, multifunctional, fully open-plan space or in a separate room, the chances are you will need to create zones for different activities. These may be anything from reading or watching TV to working on your laptop or catching up on social media. There will also be times when you'll want to share the space with friends.

I always incorporate as many different seating areas in a living space as it can comfortably accommodate without looking overfull. Several different but sympathetic arrangements result in a room that is far more dynamic and inviting than one where the furniture is arranged around the perimeter, usually facing the TV. At the very least, this might be a comfy armchair for reading, with good lighting, a side table and easy access to bookshelves; a cosy place for lounging while watching the latest boxset; and another seating area for socializing with friends, with sofas or chairs facing each other convivially over a coffee table. Each zone should have its own identity while being fully in balance with the space as a whole.

This view shows how the structural columns create a natural divide, which I decided to make use of.

Full-height pivoting panels in glossy dark lacquer divide my TV room from the main space and make beguiling reflections.

The horizontal and vertical grid lines are much in evidence. If you use the grid to inform your design, you can't go wrong.

I kept the upstairs walkway open so that it benefits from natural light and views of the ground floor.

CREATE A STRIKING VIEW FROM ALL DIRECTIONS

CHOOSING & ARRANGING FURNITURE

The style of furniture you choose for your living area is a matter of personal preference, but you need to make sure that every item you include contributes something to the scheme as a whole, so that nothing jars or seems out of place.

I tend to select furniture with its form, texture and tone foremost in my mind. I look at a piece's shape, lines and scale, its material, colour and finish, and assess whether these elements will work within my overall tonal palette and textural story. Remember, too, that you're seeking to create balance by offsetting straight lines with curves – the yang and yin of design.

OLD & NEW

Often a client will ask me to include an heirloom or a special item that they love. Sometimes that piece will become a focal point in the room and is the inspirational springboard for the entire scheme.

I love introducing unexpected juxtapositions into my designs and often find that placing an antique piece alongside a contemporary one reinvigorates it and creates a new dynamic through the contrast. It can also be rewarding to reupholster, stain or repaint a vintage item to give it a completely fresh look that works better within your scheme. This is also an opportunity to create interest with

THE FIRE OR TV IS OFTEN THE FOCAL POINT

Some chairs are almost pieces of sculpture, like this one by Gallerie 16, which tones with the photograph by Flip Schulke.

This exciting living space pivots around an iconic vintage Willy Rizzo coffee table.

contrasting textures. Unusual pairings can be extremely effective, such as covering an antique chair in leather edged with metal studs, or in natural linen with a long chain-mail fringe that drapes to the floor, or wrapping it in velvet, right down to its feet.

Bear in mind that while it's perfectly feasible to work with pieces that you already have, if an item of furniture is too big for the space, limits the layout too much or just doesn't look right, let it go. The aim is to furnish your home with pieces that excite and inspire you.

COMFORT

This really is the most important factor when you're buying furniture for lounging and relaxation. It can be very tempting to surf the Internet to find good deals on armchairs and sofas, but I'd advise you to always try before you buy such key pieces, as they should feel inviting and enveloping as well look good. And always note doorway dimensions so you know what will fit through them.

These dark oak cubes with matt brass inlays, by Azadeh Shladovsky, can be grouped together, as here, in place of a conventional coffee table, or used as stools or side tables.

PLANNING THE LAYOUT

First, decide on the number and type of zones you want to incorporate in your living space. Then work out where you'll site each one and how you'll furnish it –including lamps and power points. The best way to plan a layout and make sure everything will fit comfortably is to draw up an accurate floor plan, with windows, doors, alcoves and fireplaces all featured. Make cut-outs of each piece of furniture to the same scale and move them around on the plan to determine the best layout. Take the height of each item into account and leave plenty of breathing space to ensure you can move around freely.

The fireplace and TV are likely to be focal points of the main conversation area and lounging zone respectively. You may also want an artwork or star piece of furniture to be the focus for a sitting area. Key pieces to include are seating – sofas, armchairs, stools, ottomans – side tables, coffee tables and lighting. Every chair or sofa should have a table within easy reach.

If you're working with a large space, you may want to introduce physical boundaries between zones, in the form of pivoting or sliding screens, or display or storage units. You can also create a sense of separation through the placement of furniture – for instance, by the direction it faces or with the addition of a console table. Statement pieces can also be a great way to punctuate the space.

ALL SEATING AREAS NEED A TABLE AND GOOD LIGHTING

Every element in this pale neutral living room adds a new texture. Table nests like these glossy ones are great space-savers.

Bespoke joinery, designed for the items you want to store or display, can transform a room. This oak unit has shelves of varying depths and a sliding panel of matching plaster for textural interest.

" Furniture has a huge impact on a room's overall look and feel, so avoid spontaneous purchases and ensure you love every piece.

SEASONAL UPDATES

It can be enjoyable to reinvigorate a living room from time to time, by making a few simple changes that create a fresh new look and alter the feel of the space. The advent of a new season is a great time to do this, as it often marks a shift in lifestyle and mood.

A change in the weather has an impact on how we live and, in particular, how much time we spend indoors. Warm summer months call for outdoor living, and we want our homes to be light, cool and breezy, with a strong connection between indoors and out. As it grows cooler, we retreat indoors, to be cosy in front of the fire and to watch films on rainy weekends. There are many easy ways to give a living space a seasonal twist to reflect this change in mood.

FIREPLACES

There's nothing more welcoming on a dull, chilly day than a lit fire. Whether you make the most of a traditional fireplace or install a contemporary design or an eco wood burner, it will usually be a focal point in a living space. In summer, when it's not lit, you can create a similar atmosphere with candles.

This sleek double-aspect fireplace, screened by glass, is set low in the wall between a living room and hall so it can be enjoyed from both spaces.

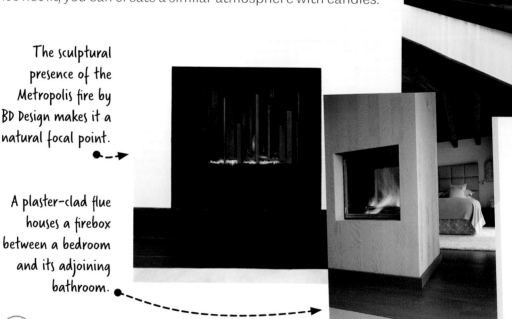

The sculptural presence of the Metropolis fire by BD Design makes it a natural focal point.

A plaster-clad flue houses a firebox between a bedroom and its adjoining bathroom.

In this glamorous living area with its marble wall panels, stunning views are enjoyed through tall glass doors that can be opened up in the summer. The air-conditioning and heating vent runs along the length of the room at ceiling level and is lit to emphasize the grid.

Ceiling coffers can discreetly incorporate air-conditioning and heating vents.

SOFT FURNISHINGS

A different set of textiles will instantly alter the mood of a living area. Summer calls for lightweight fabrics in pale, fresh hues. Come winter, throw down faux-fur rugs; add cosy throws and cushions in rich-toned velvet or wool; and replace or overlay light-filtering sheers with heavier lined curtains.

LIVING ROOM LIGHTING

Well-planned, versatile lighting enhances a living space and makes it feel inviting. It can be designed to engender different atmospheres and directed to bring out the qualities of the decorative finishes and materials used, as well as highlighting art and displays.

Nothing makes a room feel more dismal than ill-conceived lighting – picture the deadening effect of a single overhead light that casts unflattering shadows and creates gloomy corners. Lighting should be thought of as another decorative layer that accentuates the characteristics of textures, brings out nuances of colour and tone, adds a sense of theatre through light and shade, and creates a feeling of warmth.

Lighting must be planned according to the layout of the room, and the various circuits and power points installed before the wall finishes and flooring. Use the floor plan to work out where beams and pools of light need to fall. Include accent lighting for artworks, star pieces and features; beams that wash light over walls and floors so it bounces back into the room; shadow-gap lighting along skirting boards; LED strips along picture rails and under shelves; integrated lighting for display units; task lighting for reading; a mix of table and floor lamps; and a statement chandelier or pendant.

A trio of Arteinmotion pendants are hung at different levels to lower the focus in this double-height space, while the backlit shelves create warmth even when the fire is unlit.

A chandelier and pair of floor lamps create dramatic and balanced lighting.

ONE SHOW-STOPPER CREATES IMPACT

Jeremy Cole's pendant of 368 china leaves brings spiky texture
to this tonal room, while Robert Kuo's floor lamp adds shine.

PADDED HEADBOARDS
ARE A MUST

BEDROOMS

The bedroom is your private retreat, so make it as luxurious, calming and peaceful as possible, with elements to delight all the senses. It's one of the most important rooms in the home, a place in which you are likely to spend a great deal of your time – albeit largely when you're asleep – and from where you want to emerge rested and refreshed to face each day.

How you design your bedroom is very personal. Unlike the main living areas of your home, your bedroom won't be seen by visitors. It's your space, so you only need to please yourself – and, of course, anyone you share it with. The bedroom should feel like your ultimate sanctuary, so design a space that makes you feel positive, relaxed and safe, with uplifting colours, tactile fabrics, lighting that is both flattering and soothing, and objects that make you feel happy.

Eastern-inspired black linen panels partly screen the bed from view, but the eye is drawn by the fluid-looking strip of red velvet running down its centre. The tactile fabrics, including white ostrich leather, charcoal flannel and dark grey satin offset the concrete base.

BEDROOM STYLE

With the design of the master bedroom, you have more freedom to create a space that has its own personality and style, as it doesn't need to conform to the overall sense of continuity in the way the more public areas of your home do. Generally, I prefer to stick to neutral tones, as I find them so tranquil, calming and easy to live with, but a splash of a favourite colour used as an accent can be inspiring and cheering, especially on dark mornings. Greens and blues are soothing and can be quite grounding, while oranges and reds are warm, passionate hues that also work well in bedrooms.

Glamorous, sensuous materials that look wonderful and feel great against the skin are essential. Choose everything with comfort in mind – the bedroom is all about nurturing and restoring body and mind, and promoting a sense of well-being.

FURNITURE

The bedroom is for sleeping, primarily, but it may also be where you like to read, watch TV and even work. It's also likely to be the room where you dress, style your hair and apply make-up. It's vital to think about how and when you plan to use the space, so you can devise a design that works well for you.

The bed is the natural centrepiece of a bedroom and is where your focus falls when you step inside the room. Comfort is the most important factor, so always buy the best-quality bed you can afford – it's an investment that should last many years, and your back will thank you. I also recommend that

you buy the largest bed your space can accommodate without feeling cramped. Depending on the size of the room, you may not have much choice about where to position the bed. The placement of the windows, doors and fireplace, if there is one, will all play a part in this decision. As always, use the grid system to plan the layout, and ensure there is enough clear space to allow you to open doors freely and to access any storage.

In terms of other bedroom furniture, bedside tables are essential – I've used everything from vintage chests and free-standing tables or cabinets to wall-mounted designs. These may

The geometric neutral blocking, offset with upbeat orange, is contemporary and fun for a teenager's bedroom.

be conceived as extensions of the headboard itself, or as runners that continue up the wall and sometimes over the ceiling to emphasize the grid.

A dressing table is another key piece, in my view. I have a wonderful vintage design that has been with me for many years. If you can't source one that you like, a simple floating shelf with a wall-hung mirror can work just as well.

If space permits, I will often include a seating area in a bedroom. An additional chair or ottoman on which to throw clothes or extra blankets is always useful, too, and a great chance to source a one-off or statement piece.

KEEP BEDROOMS FREE FROM CLUTTER

This stylish solution in orange lacquer can be used as a dressing table or a desk, with a classic white Tulip chair by Eero Saarinen.

The defined vertical and horizontal lines — of the architecture, the desk and shelf structure and the bed — are balanced by the graphic patterns on the walls and floor, the curved Saarinen chair and the oversized circular mirror (seen opposite).

DRESSING THE BED

As it's the key element in the room, the bed is invariably my starting point when I'm designing a bedroom. It's usually the first thing you see when you walk into the room, so it needs to make an impact and define the style.

Once I've decided how I want the bed to look, and know what combinations of tones and textures I'm going to use to achieve that, the rest of the room scheme naturally starts to evolve. My main criteria is to make the bed itself look and feel as inviting, luxurious and glamorous as possible, with a rich mix of sensuous materials that feel good to the touch. The largest areas are naturally the bed cover and headboard, so I make decisions about those elements first, always thinking about texture and tactility.

HEADBOARDS

I'm a big fan of oversized headboards, which add drama and always give beds a real sense of presence. Generously padded and upholstered designs – often in leather, suede, velvet or linen – add a feeling of comfort and are a great opportunity to introduce a new texture. I often cover the bed base in the same material as the headboard to unify the design. Then I might anchor the bed on a silk or wool carpet edged with the same material to tie it all together. Some headboard designs incorporate bedside tables or cabinets, which gives a sleek, streamlined effect.

Silk and velvet add tactility to a mix of glass, brass and high-gloss lacquer.

In the perfect balance of light and dark, the wood side panels of this headboard, which incorporate bedside tables, echo the dark shutters and joinery, all offset by the pale upholstered centre panel and bed cover.

An oversized shell button is a simple accent for tonal linens.

A mouthwatering mix of linens, velvets, 'sueded' buffalo, specialist plaster, wood, shell and crystal.

This tranquil white bedroom, with accents of
chartreuse, black and chrome, was my guest
room in a former home. The textiles are a mix
of textured cottons and linens, with leather
on the headboard and Mies van der Rohe stool.
The velvet runner and cushion bands add a
pop of colour and break up the symmetry.

BED LINEN

We spend roughly a third of our lives in bed, so in my view, the mattress, bedding and bed linen are not areas to economize on. Where your comfort is concerned, spend that little bit extra and show yourself the care you deserve. Whether you prefer the softly rumpled character of linen or the fresh, crisp quality of a high thread-count cotton is a matter of personal preference. For me, it's got to be white sheets, but neutral tones of cream, taupe or pale grey also look elegant.

BED COVERS

The best way to give your bed a neat but glamorous look is with a generous-sized bed cover. Whether you sleep under a duvet or a sheet and blankets, the bed cover is a cloak of elegance that should drape beautifully and pool onto the floor. This is your show-stopper textile, so choose something sumptuous and tactile – a luxe velvet that feels soft against the skin; a self-patterned cotton that adds subtle texture; or a glazed linen with a soft sheen where it catches the light.

For extra interest, layer the bed cover with a contrasting runner. This can be a narrow or wide strip that runs horizontally or vertically. You can either introduce an accent colour or keep the scheme tonal and add a different textural layer.

CUSHIONS

The fabrics and embellishments you choose for your cushions are a huge part of the textural story. They should be selected when you've decided on the headboard and bed cover and should complement them, but bring in new textures – such as wool, silk, damask, mother-of-pearl.

Cushions can be controversial, but in my view a bed looks undressed without them. A classic configuration is two large squares at the back, followed by two smaller squares, with two rectangles in front. Contrasting bands and oversized buttons are signatures of mine, so don't miss the chance to add to the textural mix.

Khaki is a neutral in fashion, so why not in interiors? Here I've teamed it with black and white for a crisp, smart feel, in a mix of linens and velvets.

SEASONAL UPDATES

Just as we swap heavy overcoats and cosy woollens for lighter jackets and crisp cottons at the end of winter, the start of a new season means it's time to re-dress the bedroom, to give it a different look, feel and mood.

Switching the bed cover is an instant way to reflect a new season, so I always have one set of bed dressings made up for summer and another for winter. What could be a more uplifting way to mark the start of warmer weather than to put away the heavy velvets and damasks, and replace them with light, airy linens and silks? It's equally comforting, when the nights draw in, to get cosy under sumptuous, warm layers. Changing the bed runners and cushion bands also means you can easily update your bedroom colour accents with a seasonal palette.

WINDOW TREATMENTS

Echo the mood change across the rest of the room, where possible, and reinforce it with scent and flowers. Your choice of window treatment will depend on whether you like to wake up in daylight or prefer total darkness. I love shutters, as they let in light while retaining privacy. In winter you can layer shutters, blinds or gauzy sheers with drapes in weightier fabrics, which have a wonderfully cocooning effect.

Alongside an organic dish and black-and-white print by William Klein, single stems of eucalyptus foliage and scented candles bring a natural, light touch to this marble corridor.

Seasonal flowers are great ways to bring in colour, scent and natural textures. Posies and sprigs of foliage are perfect for bedrooms.

Bed runners, throws and cushions with changeable bands are a great way to dress a room in keeping with the seasons. The wide ombré runner on this elegant four-poster bed creates an East-meets-West aesthetic.

SCENT IS THE FINAL LAYER IN A BEDROOM

Neutral tones in a mix of velvet, satin and linen fabrics create such luxury.

CALM & PEACE

BEDROOM LIGHTING

The bedroom is the perfect space for magical lighting effects, so give some thought to creating enchanting plays of light and shadows on every surface, from walls and mirrors to floors and ceilings.

The bed is given prominence by the backlit slatted taupe-wood runners that extend from the wall-mounted bedside tables to the ceiling. Clusters of OCHRE glass bubbles add glamour.

As with every other room in the home, bedroom lighting needs to be flexible, dimmable and provide a combination of task, mood and statement lighting. Three or four circuits should provide you with the versatility to change the ambience from uplifting and energizing in the morning while you're getting up, to tranquil and relaxing in the evening as you're winding down towards sleep.

Low-level lighting is a practical option for bedrooms, as this will guide you around safely if you get up during the night. You will also need task lighting for reading – over the bed, a seating area, or both – and at your dressing table. Side lighting is more flattering than an overhead light for vanity areas.

USE LIGHT TO EMPHASIZE THE GRID

LIGHT EFFECTS

The ceiling in the bedroom is seen more than any other in the home, so why not bring light into play to make a feature of it? Chandeliers, crystal lights and points of light will all create subtle patterns, while uplights and directional spotlights will cast beams of light where you want them and throw dramatic shadows. Architectural lighting, which can be installed in a ceiling coffer or along the top of built-in cupboards, will give both ceiling and walls a warm glow.

Like crystal waterfalls, these beautiful pendants throw a magical pattern of light and shadows onto the runners of specialist plaster on either side of the leather bed I designed.

Jeremy Cole's porcelain Aloe Shoot pendants stand out against the joinery that frames the bed and separates the bedroom from a dressing room. The headboard is pale linen, to tone with the velvet bed cover, and on the reverse is a mirror.

A glass pendant from Lasvit highlights an array of textures — wood, marble, fabrics, leather and wallpaper.

Drama can be created by directing beams of accent light onto architectural features, focal points, art or specialist finishes. Throwing gentle washes of light onto surfaces and finishes also creates stunning effects by enhancing their characteristics and accentuating textural contrasts. You can also underlight built-in cupboards or shelves, or backlight niches, display units and slatted runners – a dramatic way to emphasize the grid.

Remember that the materials, colours and finishes you choose for your décor will have a direct bearing on the quality and behaviour of light. Dark, matt surfaces absorb light and create a cosy, nurturing environment, while paler colours and shiny surfaces reflect light and bounce it around the room.

BEDSIDE LIGHTS

With so many elegant, dramatic and decorative designs to choose from, bedside lights are often the stars of the show and set the mood. Statement lights on either side of the bed give it a sense of presence. They also create symmetry – even more so when they are hung or placed in front of a grid-defining wall runner in a contrasting material.

One of my favourite ways to add glamour and impact is to hang fabulous pendants beside the bed instead of lamps – also saving table space. Cascading crystals, sleek glass cylinders, clusters of glass bubbles, shiny metal globes and porcelain sculptures are just some of my favourites.

The opulent feel of this bedroom is brought about by the rich mix of textures and the way these are enhanced by the lighting. The cascading crystal pendants cast patterns of shadows on the runners of taupe specialist plaster, while the underlit bedside ledges gleam and glow.

> Plan the lighting around your layout, so you end up with the right light options exactly where you need them.

ALWAYS INCLUDE A GLAMOROUS LIGHT

STORAGE

Bedroom storage – whether it's integrated into the main sleeping area or in a separate dressing room – should be planned with precision, so that everything has a home and you can find the items you want with ease.

GOOD LIGHTING IS ESSENTIAL IN DRESSING AREAS

Try to keep your bedroom tidy and clutter-free. It's the simplest way to make the space calming and conducive to rest.

Separate dressing areas are a wonderful but practical luxury if you have the space. For convenience, they should ideally be located in an adjoining space or partitioned off from the main sleeping area. A solution I often design is a double-sided structure that incorporates the headboard with built-in bedside tables on one side, and a storage unit or large mirror on the other.

The décor in a dressing room should echo that of the main bedroom with regard to the materials, textures and tones used, to unify the two spaces visually. But I also like to add a touch of glamour. My own dressing room has the atmosphere of a luxury atelier, with blush-pink velvet-covered chairs, fresh flowers

Stained oak-veneer was used for this bespoke mix of open and closed storage, including an island unit of drawers with a built-in velvet-covered seat. The space benefits from natural light, but integral lighting highlights the collection of bags.

and black-and-white photography on the walls. It's a good idea to have at least one chair or ottoman to place clothes on when you're getting changed, and to make it easier to put on boots and shoes. Make sure you have really good lighting and large mirrors, so you can check your outfit with a critical gaze from all angles before facing the world.

If there isn't room to have a separate dressing area, assess your bedroom for storage opportunities and decide on the best ways to make use of every nook and cranny – from awkward spaces under the eaves, to alcoves, to the spaces around and above the bed. Built-in storage provides the most streamlined look and usually makes the best use of space, with the interior customized to suit your needs.

There is a huge range of good-quality ready-made storage systems available, which you can easily personalize by changing the handles or knobs. Another, albeit more expensive, option is to have your storage solutions designed from scratch, to your exact specifications. I always approach bedroom storage with the same attention to detail as kitchen design. Careful planning from the outset really does pay off, and you'll be surprised by just how much a well-designed storage unit can hold.

The dark-chocolate tones of the built-in cupboards, bedside tables and shutters create an elegant and cocooning atmosphere.

Floor-to-ceiling cupboards utilize every bit of available space and give a streamlined effect. These slatted Eastern-style doors look smart and add textural interest.

ASSESSING YOUR NEEDS

The first step to designing efficient bedroom storage that meets all your requirements is to assess your belongings – this is a great opportunity to clear out any tired or unworn items. First think about the broad categories – underwear, tops, knitwear, activewear, and so on. Some items need to be within easy reach on a daily basis, others may only be worn occasionally so don't have to be quite so accessible. Shoes, boots, hats, belts and bags all require different storage solutions from long dresses, shirts, jumpers and trousers. Decide whether you want a mix of open and closed storage, and what configuration of hanging space, shelves, drawers and pull-out racks you require.

CHOOSE HANDLES THAT MAKE A STYLE STATEMENT

Slim, pencil-like drawer handles in decorative fixings emphasize the horizontal lines of the grid.

A dressing area or bedroom is the perfect home for a one-off chair, such as this reupholstered metal-framed 1960s design.

Door handles are a great way to add textural contrast and top-quality detailing. These handles on a dark wood cupboard have been covered in matching leather with visible stitching.

STORAGE STYLE

Think about your storage in the same way as you would any other design element in the room. A wall of built-in storage will be a dominant feature, so choose the material and detailing, including the handles, with that in mind and make sure they complement the rest of the design scheme. Wood is the obvious choice and offers a wide range of tones and textures, as smooth, slatted or panelled surfaces. There are also various materials – such as veneer, lacquer, vellum, linen, leather, glass, mirror, mother-of-pearl, brass, nickel or chrome – that can be incorporated as insets, runners or panels.

BATHROOMS

I've always been hugely influenced by the traditional Japanese bathing ritual of an invigorating cleanse followed by a relaxing soak in a warm bath, so I always design bathrooms with this in mind. Bathrooms are functional spaces, but they should also be tranquil temples where you can unwind, surrounded by cool surfaces, warm lighting, delicious scents and soft towels.

Bathrooms are expensive to replace, so it's important to do the groundwork at the start to make sure you design a space that meets your needs on both a practical and an aesthetic level. It's also essential that the fittings and fixtures are installed professionally, with due consideration given to the necessary infrastructure – including the plumbing, drainage, water pressure, location of soil pipes, strengthening of floor joists, tanking and waterproofing.

The bathtub, basin and taps are the sculptures of the bathroom, so choose designs that have a wow factor.

PLANNING A BATHROOM

As with any space you are designing, the first thing to think about is who is going to use the space, what they want from it and where it is going to be located. Moving a bathroom into a different room can cause a lot of expense and upheaval, so if this is your intention, you must take advice from your contractor about the practicalities of rerouting soil pipes, providing adequate ventilation, ensuring a water flow that is powerful enough for a shower, strengthening floor joists that may be required to support heavy materials as well as a full bathtub, and so on. This is also the case if you are planning on carving out a portion of a bedroom or hallway to make an en suite. In this case, if the new space doesn't benefit from natural light, consider whether you could incorporate 'borrowed' light into your design. Shoji panels or walls of etched or opaque glass will offer privacy without blocking out all the natural light from the adjoining area.

The sculptural bathtub, which I designed for Apaiser, is in prime position to take in views of the city skyline while enjoying a relaxing soak. The walls and floor are clad in Calacatta marble with accents of brass for added opulence.

MAKE THE BATHTUB
THE CENTREPIECE

Now is also the time to decide whether you want to include an audiovisual system, to give you music and/or TV to enjoy from the comfort of your tub, and underfloor heating, which is usually a very welcome addition in a room with so many cool surfaces. Storage is also an important element, as a messy, cluttered bathroom will not promote a state of relaxation.

A family bathroom is likely to have very different practical considerations and design criteria from a master en suite, which will naturally be a more private space. The size of the area you are working with is also a determining factor in what you can fit into it and how you design it. To ensure your bathroom meets your needs, start by asking yourself the following questions:

• How many people will be using the bathroom and what ages are they?

• Do you want a shower, a bath or both? If the latter, will you have to settle for an over-bath design or is there room for a free-standing shower, either walk-in or a wet area?

• Will taps be wall- or floor-mounted, or integrated into the bath and basin?

• How many basins would you like? Will they be free-standing or in a vanity unit that incorporates storage?

• Do you want a concealed loo cistern, with storage or niches for display?

An oversized round mirror creates a feeling of openness and is a playful balance to the lines of the angular wall-mounted basin and units below.

The dramatic use of marble for the walls, floor and chunky sinks creates an illusion of space in this magnificent bathroom.

JUXTAPOSE MATERIALS TO BRING DESIGNS TO LIFE

A runner of pebbles bound in resin is set into the white Thassos stone wall of this shower cubicle, with the same materials repeated on the floor. The glossy white-lacquered vanity unit contrasts with the matt surface of the dark wood door.

BATHROOM LIGHTING

Lighting is a wonderful design tool in a bathroom. As well as task lighting for practical purposes, light can be used decoratively by bouncing it off surfaces to enhance the qualities of the textures and materials, and to make the most of glossy, reflective finishes.

SOFT LIGHT WILL ADD WARMTH AND COMFORT TO A BATHROOM

This pendant light by In-es.artdesign and side tables by Hamilton Conte add texture and a decorative, playful element to this bathroom.

A soft, warm glow of light reflects off the milk-glass bath surround. The taps, my own design for Waterfront, are mounted on a backlit marble panel that makes them appear to float while defining the lines of the space.

Successful bathroom lighting provides a versatile combination of general, task and ambient light. Usually, three separate circuits, with dimmers, will give you sufficient control to switch the mood from cheering and vitalizing, for when you are getting ready for the day in a hurry, to mellow and soothing, for when you want to unwind with a soak in the bath before bed.

Task lighting is generally needed at the vanity unit, for shaving or applying make-up. Avoid overhead lighting here, as it will cast shadows onto your face. More flattering options include gentle side lighting from vertical fittings on each side of the mirror,

non-fluorescent light integrated within it, or indirect uplighting that bounces light off the ceiling.

Concealed low-level lighting washes the floor in a gentle glow and highlights textures and finishes, while uplighters and directional spotlights do the same for ceilings and walls. Underlighting the base of vanity or storage units makes them appear to float, at the same time defining the grid. A similar result is achieved by backlighting a 'floating' wall panel. Positioning such a panel behind a bathtub gives the star feature in the room a greater sense of presence. Backlit shelves and niches also add to the decorative effect.

Three Lee Broom crystal and brass pendants hang over an oak shelf stained to match the marble's veins.

The Petite Friture pendant echoes the Apaiser bath I designed; the niches and shower are lit by recessed downlights.

CLEANSE & REJUVENATE

Bathrooms have two main functions. First and foremost they're places to wash and refresh in readiness for the day ahead, but the same spaces are also used for relaxation and pampering.

To ensure your bathroom is successful in fulfilling both of these roles, the fittings and other elements that you choose, together with the layout that you design, need to be conducive to these different activities and moods. Good plumbing, lighting and heating, practical surfaces and comfortable fittings are all bathroom essentials, but so are the other aspects that contribute to engendering a serene and tranquil atmosphere.

FIXTURES & FITTINGS

Refer back to your list of priorities and specifications, and then visit as many suppliers and showrooms as you can to choose the elements that will fulfil your brief and suit your budget. You don't have to buy everything from the same place – as long as the items you choose work together visually – but you'll need to coordinate deliveries to make sure your contractors have what they need when they need it.

Arabescato marble, grey plasterwork, black wood and white fittings create a smart balance of tones and textures.

Marble adds soft colour, natural patterning and a sense of luxury to walls and floors.

If you love bathing, it's worth allocating a sizeable portion of your budget to buy a bathtub that will be the sculptural centrepiece of your bathroom. Put any self-consciousness aside and lie down in it in the showroom to make sure it's comfortable and a good length and depth for you.

The Origami bath I designed for Apaiser, with taps mounted in a marble block, complements the black timber trelliswork screen behind, creating layers of texture, all softened by the addition of flowers.

The floor-standing origami sink is one of my designs for Apaiser, here set on a grey-toned wood floor that echoes the veins of the marble walls. The mirror and black lacquer runner add shiny contrast.

The white double sink pops against the graphic Striato Olimpico marble, creating a feeling of excitement in this contemporary bathroom.

Marble is one of my favourite materials to use in bathrooms, as it adds soft tones, subtle patterning, natural texture and glamour.

My Apaiser Harmony bath, made from reclaimed marble, was inspired by a collection of bowls I designed for Wedgwood. The Calacatta marble plinth is echoed by the wall runner in the shower enclosure.

If a bathtub isn't your priority, apportion more of the budget to a really luxurious shower. There are so many great designs that offer all manner of shower heads and spa jets to enhance your cleansing experience. Make the shower enclosure as spacious as possible, with plenty of room to move around without knocking your elbows. A luxurious wall material in the shower enclosure – such as specialist plaster, stone or marble cladding – always has an impact, but you can also create stunning effects with less expensive tiles – from large slabs to mosaics – or with laminate, acrylic or resin panels.

If your budget is tight, you could buy the rest of the sanitaryware from a cheaper but complementary range, but one thing I always advise is not to skimp on taps. They are the works of art in bathroom design, and a beautifully designed tap in whatever finish you desire – from cool chrome to statement brass – will set the tone of the bathroom and make it feel instantly more luxurious and special.

Floor-standing basins are ideal for cloakrooms or where there is room for separate bathroom storage. But a built-in vanity unit, with one or two sinks, is practical and can also be very stylish in glossy lacquer, wood, stone, marble or a composite material.

This organic stone sink offsets the lines of the dark wood shelf and mirror runner.

On an underlit plinth of Calacatta marble in the centre of the taupe wood floor, this bathtub is the focal point of my bathroom.

BATHROOMS MUST BE AS LUXURIOUS AS POSSIBLE

RELAX & UNWIND

Mood lighting plays a significant role in creating an instant change of atmosphere and promoting relaxation, but the overall design of the bathroom, and the fittings, fixtures and materials you choose to surround yourself with, also generate a feeling of calm.

In a former bathroom of mine, light-reflecting taupe milk glass was used for the bath surround and flooring, with an inset runner of black oak defining the grid and drawing focus to the tub.

Carrara marble clads both the walls and floor of this bathroom, with its simple but strikingly graphic bath.

As with any room you design, the selection of materials, tones, finishes and shapes you're drawn to include in your bathroom should be ones that delight and inspire you, that lift your spirits and give you pleasure to look at, to use and to touch. If you don't choose all of these elements with care and thought, no amount of tranquil lighting will make you feel relaxed in the space. If the bathtub is uncomfortable to lie back in, if the shower isn't powerful enough, the basin isn't large enough or the stone flooring looks too grey against the marble wall, it will always niggle you and make you feel on edge.

CHOOSING MATERIALS

The choice of materials for bathrooms can feel overwhelming – for the main surfaces and joinery, but even for elements such as sinks, which come in everything from ceramic, glass, stone and marble to various composites. My golden rule that I invariably follow is to use three materials, one of which will always be mirror, plus the wall finish. Some of my favourite materials to use in bathrooms are:

● Mirror – an essential material in every bathroom, both for practical reasons and as a light-reflecting tool

● Marble – for walls, floors or sinks, or all three; preferably Carrara, Arabescato or Calacatta

● Glass – usually clear or coloured milk glass (a painted foil-backed reinforced glass)

● Wood – oak, either natural or stained taupe, grey or black

● Stone – rough-hewn or polished, or a combination of the two

● Specialist plaster – a number of finishes can be achieved from polished plaster to textured finishes incorporating colour pigment

Combinations that I find especially successful and that I've turned to time and again in bathroom designs are:

● Mirror with stone and wood
● Mirror with glass and wood
● Mirror with marble and wood
● Mirror with rubber and wood
● Mirror with marble and resin

A white egg-shaped bath is a sculptural presence against the backdrop of grey-veined Arabescato marble that clads both the walls and floor. Its graceful curves balance the lines of the room, the inset niche and the TV screen.

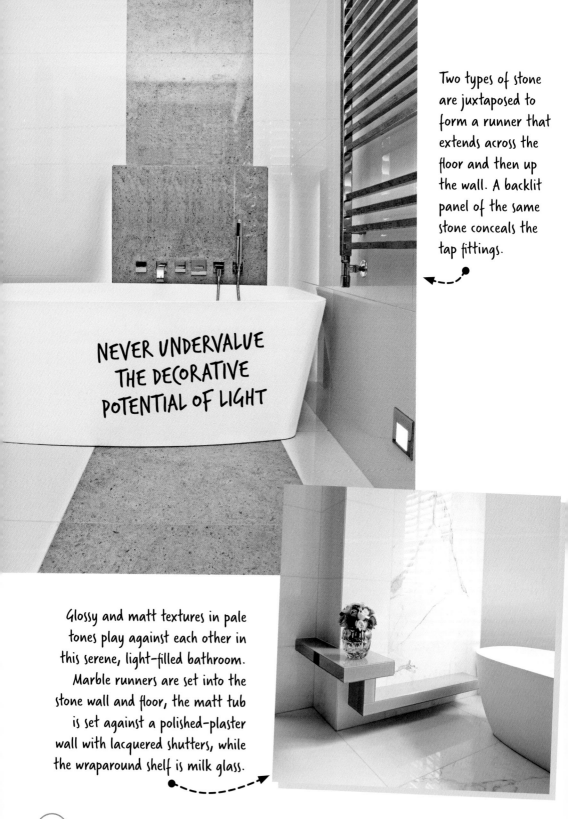

Two types of stone are juxtaposed to form a runner that extends across the floor and then up the wall. A backlit panel of the same stone conceals the tap fittings.

NEVER UNDERVALUE THE DECORATIVE POTENTIAL OF LIGHT

Glossy and matt textures in pale tones play against each other in this serene, light-filled bathroom. Marble runners are set into the stone wall and floor, the matt tub is set against a polished-plaster wall with lacquered shutters, while the wraparound shelf is milk glass.

DESIGNING THE LAYOUT

Once you've decided on the elements you want to include in your bathroom, plan the layout using the grid system to impose structure (see page 22). The easiest way to decide on the best configuration is to use a floor plan, drawn to scale, with cut-outs of the bathroom fixtures and fittings you want to include, also drawn to the same scale. You can simply move these around on the plan until you come to an arrangement you're happy with.

Key things to consider are the views you'll create – both as you enter the room and as seen from the bathtub. Ideally, you want the statement tub or a star basin to be the main focal point of the room and the first thing your eye is drawn to as you walk in, not the loo. If there's a view from a window, position the bath to take advantage of it – unless you're planning a TV inset into a wall.

The bathroom must be timeless, not fashion-led, and achieve a perfect balance of practicality and aspiration, function and beauty.

My ideal bathroom includes:

- A stand-out bathtub that takes centre stage

- Two basins – a practical solution to the morning rush

- A powerful shower in a spacious enclosure

- A stylish and discreetly positioned loo

- Bespoke storage, including niches for display

- Flexible lighting that's flattering, decorative and functional

- A wonderful mix of materials that combines matt and gloss textures and creates a glamorous, opulent feel

CONTRASTING RUNNERS

When you've decided on the optimum layout, refer to the mix of materials on your design board and think about where you can introduce contrasting runners. Could the mirror over the basin be a floor-to-ceiling runner, or a horizontal strip across the whole wall behind a two-basin vanity unit? I often set a runner into the floor leading from the door to the basin, or from the basin to the bathtub. You could then extend this up the wall behind the bath, or add a backlit panel – the possibilities are endless.

STORAGE

The relaxing effects of any bathroom, however well designed and lit, will be ruined in an instant if there is visible clutter or unsightly containers on show. How much storage you allow for will depend on how big the bathroom is, but always include somewhere to stash spare loo rolls, soap, shampoo and so on. Cupboards can be cleverly hidden behind contrasting runners or built into niches above a concealed cistern or under the sink. Make the best use of space by sourcing uniform containers scaled to fit small items such as cotton balls or buds. Floating shelves are elegant, define the grid and offer display points for candles, plants, attractive bottles of bath oil and neatly folded towels.

FINISHING TOUCHES

If your bathroom is large enough, consider adding a chair, stool or side table, especially if you have a free-standing bathtub without a handy ledge to rest a drink or a book on.

Flowers add a feminine touch and soften the effect of all the hard surfaces and sharp lines. Plants are also wonderful natural additions to bathrooms and many, such as ferns, thrive in a warm, steamy atmosphere.

Scent is an essential ingredient for a relaxing bathroom, whether in the form of diffusers, room sprays, bath oils or scented candles, which give the added bonus of soft, soothing light.

The roomy glass shower enclosure allows views of the striking linear shower head and boldly patterned marble wall. The towel rail is conveniently located on one side of it, with the TV on the other, at the perfect height to be viewed from the bath.

A runner of glass mosaic cuts centrally through the Calacatta marble floor between the egg-shaped bath and the rectangular sink, which has floating oak shelves on either side of it to create balance.

INDEX

Page numbers in *italics* refer to illustrations

Other titles available by Kelly Hoppen

House of Hoppen
Kelly Hoppen Design Masterclass
Kelly Hoppen Ideas
Kelly Hoppen Home
Kelly Hoppen Style

www.kellyhoppen.co.uk
www.kellyhoppen.asia

Instagram @kellyhoppen
Twitter @kellyhoppen
LinkedIn @kellyhoppeninteriors

ACKNOWLEDGEMENTS

Every effort has been made to trace copyright holders of artworks, designs and photography. We apologize in advance for any unintentional omissions and would be pleased to insert the appropriate acknowledgements in any subsequent publication.

Photography Credits:
2–3 Malcolm Menzies © 6–7 Pavel Jovik © 8–9 Mike Toy © (www.miketoy.com) 11 Jacqui Small © (photographer: Mel Yates) 12 Mel Yates © 14-15 Kelly Hoppen Interiors © (photographer: Steve Leung) 16 Jacqui Small © (photographer: Mel Yates) 19 Thomas Stewart © 20 Jacqui Small © (photographer: Mel Yates) 21 Kelly Hoppen Interiors © (photographer: Steve Leung) 22–23 Nang Fung Developments © 24 Mel Yates © 26 Mel Yates © 27 Mel Yates © 28 Chen Wei Zhong © 28–29 Mel Yates © 29 Bill Batten © 30t Nang Fung Developments © 30–31 Pavel Jovik © 33 Si-Cong Sui © 34–35 Mel Yates © 37 Bill Batten © 38 Jacqui Small © (photographer: Mel Yates) 40–41 Thomas Stewart © 42t Jacqui Small © (photographer: Mel Yates) 44–45 Jacqui Small © (photographer: Mel Yates) 46t Si-Cong Sui © 46b Si-Cong Sui © 48t Mel Yates © 48b Mel Yates © 50t Mel Yates © 52t Yoo Lodha Estrella © 52b Nang Fung Developments © 54t Jacqui Small © (photographer: Mel Yates) 54c Jacqui Small © (photographer: Mel Yates) 54b 56–57 Mel Yates © 58t Kelly Hoppen Interiors © (photographer: Steve Leung) 58b Jacqui Small © (photographer: Mel Yates) 59t Mel Yates © 59bl Jacqui Small © (photographer: Vincent Knapp) 59br Jacqui Small © (photographer: Mel Yates) 60t Jacqui Small © (photographer: Mel Yates) 60b Jacqui Small © (photographer: Vincent Knapp) 61t Jacqui Small © (photographer: Mel Yates) 61bl Mel Yates © 61br Thomas Stewart © 62t Mel Yates © 62bl client's own 62br Jacqui Small © (photographer: Vincent Knapp) 63tl Mel Yates © 63r Bill Batten © 63bl Jacqui Small © (photographer: Vincent Knapp) 64t Mel Yates © 64b Thomas Stewart © 65tl Mel Yates © 65tr Jacqui Small © (photographer: Mel Yates) 65c Mel Yates © 65b Thomas Stewart © 66 Jacqui Small © (photographer: Vincent Knapp) 69 Jacqui Small © (photographer: Mel Yates) 70 Mel Yates © 71 Jacqui Small

© (photographer: Mel Yates) 72 Mel Yates © 73t Mel Yates © 73c Mel Yates © 73b Mel Yates © 74l Jacqui Small © (photographer: Mel Yates) 74r Jacqui Small © (photographer: Vincent Knapp) 74–75 Simon Upton/Interior Archive, Simon Upton/TIA Digital Ltd 75bl Jacqui Small © (photographer: Mel Yates) 75r Jacqui Small © (photographer: Mel Yates) 76 Jacqui Small © (photographer: Mel Yates) 77l Jacqui Small © (photographer: Mel Yates) 77r Jacqui Small © (photographer: Vincent Knapp) 78 Regal London ©79t Jacqui Small © (photographer: Mel Yates) 79r Mel Yates © 79bl Jacqui Small © (photographer: Vincent Knapp) 80–81 Jacqui Small © (photographer: Mel Yates) 82 Jacqui Small © (photographer: Mel Yates) 82–83 Jacqui Small © (photographer: Mel Yates) 83b Jacqui Small © (photographer: Vincent Knapp) 83r Jacqui Small © (photographer: Mel Yates) 84–85 Mel Yates © 86–87 Malcolm Menzies © 89tl Mel Yates © 89bl Mel Yates © 89tr Mel Yates © 89br Chen Wei Zhong © 91 Si-Cong Sui © 92 Jacqui Small © (photographer: Mel Yates) 94l Jacqui Small © (photographer: Mel Yates) 94r Jin Yi Qi © 95l Mel Yates © 95r Si-Cong Sui © 96 Mel Yates © 97 Yoo Lodha Estrella © 98t Si-Cong Sui © 98b Nang Fung Developments © 99l Si-Cong Sui © 99r Si-Cong Sui © 100 Mel Yates © 101l Mel Yates © 101r Kelly Hoppen Interiors © (photographer: Steve Leung) 102 Jacqui Small © (photographer: Mel Yates) 103 Mel Yates © 104t Jacqui Small © (photographer: Mel Yates) 104ml Mel Yates © 104mr Jacqui Small © (photographer: Mel Yates) 104b Jacqui Small © (photographer: Mel Yates) 105 clockwise from top left Mel Yates ©, Jacqui Small © (photographer: Mel Yates), Jacqui Small © (photographer: Mel Yates), Mel Yates ©, Jacqui Small © (photographer: Mel Yates), Jacqui Small © (photographer: Mel Yates) 106 Jacqui Small © (photographer: Mel Yates) 107 Jacqui Small © (photographer: Vincent Knapp) 109 Jacqui Small © (photographer: Mel Yates) 110l Jacqui Small © (photographer: Mel Yates) 110m Jacqui Small © (photographer: Mel Yates) 110r Photographer Chen Wei Zhong 111l Jacqui Small © (photographer: Mel Yates) 111r Mel Yates © 112t Jacqui Small © (photographer: Vincent Knapp) 112b Mel Yates © 113t Photographer Mel Yates 113b Jacqui Small © (photographer: Mel Yates) 114 Mel Yates

© 115tl Jacqui Small © (photographer: Mel Yates) 115tr Mel Yates © 115bl Jacqui Small © (photographer: Mel Yates) 115br Jacqui Small © (photographer: Mel Yates) 116 Photographer Mel Yates 118l Photographer Chen Wei Zhong 118r Mel Yates © 119l Kelly Hoppen Interiors © (photographer: Steve Leung) 120 Thomas Stewart © 121l Bill Batten © 121r Topwin Development Ltd © 122 Kelly Hoppen Interiors © (photographer: Steve Leung) 123t Kelly Hoppen Interiors © (photographer: Steve Leung) 123b Photographer Mel Yates 124tl Photographer Si Cong Sui 124tr Photographer Si Cong Sui 124bl Photographer Si Cong Sui 124br Photographer Si Cong Sui 125b Jacqui Small © (photographer: Vincent Knapp) 126l Mel Yates © 126r Mel Yates © 127 Mel Yates © 128 Yoo Lodha Estrella © 130 Mel Yates © 133 Jacqui Small © (photographer: Vincent Knapp) 134l Jacqui Small © (photographer: Vincent Knapp) 134r Jacqui Small © (photographer: Mel Yates) 135l Mel Yates © 135r Photographer Si Cong Sui 136–137 Mel Yates © 138 Jacqui Small © (photographer: Mel Yates) 139 Jacqui Small © (photographer: Vincent Knapp) 140t Jacqui Small © (photographer: Mel Yates) 140b Jacqui Small © (photographer: Vincent Knapp) 141t Jacqui Small © (photographer: Mel Yates) 141b Simon Upton/Interior Archive; Simon Upton/ TIA Digital Ltd © 142 Jacqui Small © (photographer: Vincent Knapp) 143 Jacqui Small © (photographer: Mel Yates) 144 Mel Yates © 146–147 Mel Yates © 148–149 Mel Yates © 150 Yoo Lodha Estrella © 151 Jacqui Small © (photographer: Mel Yates) 152–153 Jacqui Small © (photographer: Mel Yates) 154–155 Mel Yates © 156–157 Mel Yates © 158–159 Mel Yates © 160 Mel Yates © 161t Photographer Mel Yates 161b Kelly Hoppen Interiors © (photographer: Steve Leung) 162–163 Jacqui Small © (photographer: Mel Yates) 164l Jacqui Small © (photographer: Mel Yates) 164r Photographer Mel Yates 165t Kelly Hoppen Interiors © (photographer: Steve Leung) 165m Jacqui Small © (photographer: Mel Yates) 165b Photographer Chen Wei Zhong 166l Photographer Si Cong Sui 166r Mel Yates © 167 Mel Yates © 168 Thomas Stewart © 170 Photographer Jin Yi Qi 171 Photographer Jin Yi Qi 172l Photographer Chen Wei Zhong 172r Mel Yates 173t Jacqui Small © (photographer: Mel Yates) 173b Mel Yates © 174 Jacqui

Small © (photographer: Mel Yates) 175 Mel Yates © 176 Photographer Jin Yi Qi 177t Photographer Jin Yi Qi 177b Photographer Mel Yates 178 Mel Yates © 179t Jacqui Small © (photographer: Mel Yates) 179m Jacqui Small © (photographer: Mel Yates) 179b Yoo Lodha Estrella © 181 Jacqui Small © (photographer: Mel Yates) 182 Jacqui Small © (photographer: Mel Yates) 184t Mel Yates © 184b Jacqui Small © (photographer: Vincent Knapp) 185tl Jacqui Small © (photographer: Vincent Knapp) 185tr Jacqui Small © (photographer: Mel Yates) 185b Jacqui Small © (photographer: Vincent Knapp) 187 Kelly Hoppen Interiors © (photographer: Steve Leung) 188 Photographer Chen Wei Zhong 189t Jacqui Small © (photographer: Mel Yates) 189b Photographer Chen Wei Zhong 190l Jacqui Small © (photographer: Mel Yates) 190r Photographer Chen Wei Zhong 191l Mel Yates © 191r Matt Livey © 192l Jacqui Small © (photographer: Mel Yates) 192r Photographer Chen Wei Zhong 192b Mel Yates © 193l Mel Yates © 193r Photographer Si Cong Sui 194t Mel Yates © 194b Jacqui Small © (photographer: Mel Yates) 195 Mel Yates © 196–197 Jacqui Small © (photographer: Mel Yates) 198 Jacqui Small © (photographer: Mel Yates) 201 Jacqui Small © (photographer: Mel Yates)

Artist Credits:

24 artworks by Kimiko Yoshida; 27 sculpture by Paul Vanstone 40–41 photograph, Accordionist, Esztergom, October 21, 1916, by André Kertész 42t artwork by Ben Vautier 50t artwork, private collection (client's own) 60b artwork by Peter Beard (Michael Hoppen Gallery 61br photograph, Glenn Close (1994) by Herb Ritts/Trunk Archive 63bl artwork by Erro, © ADAGP, Paris and DACS, London 2016 65tl artwork by Ernst Haas, Route 66 Albuquerque (Getty Images) 70l photograph, Ali Underwater by Flip Schulke (Michael Hoppen Gallery); photograph by Duffy © Duffy Archive 71 shelf by Zaha Hadid, 'Dune 01', 2007, Editions David Gill, London; artwork by Nabil Nahas 74–75 photograph by Karl Blossfeldt © Karl Blossfeldt, Archiv Ann und Jürgen Wilde, Zülpich 95l photograph by Ellen von Unwerth/courtesy Staley-Wise Gallery, New York 102r bust, La Fanciulla by Ralph Brown 104mr Jibby Beane by Nadav Kander 104b artwork by Daniel Kelly of Kyoto, Japan, I Am Not a Geisha (2006), lithograph, woodblock, hand-colouring on paper 105tl artwork by Peter Beard 105br photograph by David Parker 107 photograph by Désirée Dolron, Grimm Gallery, Amsterdam 123t Page 245 photographs, From a Window of the Louvre by Tom Artin (left); A Bout de Souffle – Jean Seberg (Boulevard Saint-Germain) by Raymond Cauchetier, Gelatin Silver Print, 1959 (James Hyman Gallery), www.raymondcauchetier-photographs.com (right) 126r antique-copper snail by Robert Kuo 127 photograph, Kelly Hoppen by David Bailey 128, 150 artwork by Stuart Redler 130 Portrait of Marilyn Monroe in a Black Dress, c.1950, to promote The Asphalt Jungle, photograph by Ed Clark/The LIFE Picture Collection/Getty 134l artwork by Peter Beard 140t photographs by Simon Brown from the Kelly Hoppen range 140b gelatine silver collection print by Jean Baptiste Huynh 144b bronze sculpture, Hare by Barry Flanagan 147b (left to right) photograph, Ali Underwater by Flip Schulke (Michael Hoppen Gallery); photograph by Duffy © Duffy Archive; photograph, Brigitte Bardot © Terry O'Neill/courtesy of Richard Goodall Gallery; artwork by Ben Vautier; photographs, Norma Shearer by George Hurrell (Getty Images); Steve McQueen by William Claxton/courtesy Demont Photo Management; artwork by Kimiko Yoshida 165t Ablution from 'The Barking Wall', 2010, by Brendan George Ko 167 photographs by Ron van Dongen 178 photograph by Ellen von Unwerth/courtesy Staley-Wise Gallery, New York

Design Credits:

11 chainmail pendant light by Terzani 14–15 Revolve table lamp by Bert Frank 16 metal-base floor lamps, nest of sidetables, Copper Empire Drumstools (back left of image) and coffee table (back right of image) by Robert Kuo, figurative floor lamps by Porta Romana, vintage coffee tables by Kelly Hoppen (foreground), bowls by Anna Torfs 28–29 shelf unit by Kelly Hoppen 94l Aloe Shoot ceramic pendant light by Jeremy Cole 30t Albedo table lamp by Lahumière Design 34–35 Fluid pendant lights by Beau McClellan, table by Bellavista, chairs by Holly Hunt, benches from St Paul Home, carver chairs by Munna 38 frame chair by Baltus 40–41 tall wenge tables by Modénature 48t sofa by Promemoria, ceiling lights by Fortuny Scheherazade, custom-made chandelier by OCHRE 50t Rock table by Hudson Furniture, armchair by Christian Liaigre 52t 21.7 pendant lights by Bocci, bedside table and Bardot bed by Meridiani, vase by C best 55c banquettes by Kelly Hoppen 57 cupboard by Moissonnier, table lamp by Porta Romana 58t bowl from Apparatus Studio 58b vases by kellyhoppen.com 60b Saline daybed by Christian Liaigre, wooden vessel from Concho Bay 61bl bronze side table by Asiatides, cushion from Fortuny 61br Fortuny silk chair cover 62t chandelier by Beau McClellan, bookcase by Moissonnier, table by Bellavista, carver chairs by Munna, chairs by Holly Hunt, benches by St Paul Home, wall light by Promemoria 62bl Atollo table lamp by Vico Magistretti 63tl kilim by The Rug Company 63r studded wenge cabinet from David Gill Gallery 63bl chest of drawers by Garouste & Bonetti/courtesy of the David Gill Gallery 64t armchair by Massant in red leather from Garrett Leather, wall lamp from La Lampe Gras, side table by Holly Hunt, bed and bedside table by Meridiani 65tl armchair by Massant in red leather from Garrett Leather, wall lamp from La Lampe Gras, side table by Holly Hunt, bed and bedside table by Meridiani 65b rug by Kelly Hoppen 69 storage system by Kelly Hoppen for Smallbone 70l bubble pendant lights (foreground) by Kelly Hoppen with glass blown by DARK, pendant lights by Hervé Langlais for Galerie Negropontes, bespoke table designed by Kelly Hoppen with bronze base by Matt Stanwix 76 screen by Monpas 79tl Bombato mirror by Davide Medri 80r Flibuste pedestal tables by Christian Liaigre 82 table by St Paul Home, acrylic Saturn chairs Andrew Martin 82–83 hand-blown glass bubbles by Melogranoblu 83b glass Ghost chair by Cini Boeri for Fiam 85 vintage Bubble-style chairs by Kelly Hoppen Interiors, coffee tables by Kelly Hoppen, organic-shaped side table by Robert Kuo 96 wall light by Tristan Auer for Pouenat 89t stools by Tom Dixon 95l Aloe Shoot ceramic pendant light by Jeremy Cole 97 TAO Pouf by La Fibule 102l pendant lights by Kevin Reilly 103 custom-made cabinet by Smith & Brown Cabinetmakers Ltd 104t bespoke chandelier by Mark Brazier-Jones 104ml table by Robert Kuo, light by Hudson 104mr Kelly Light Sculpture by Kelly Hoppen for Spina 104b Lustre Ovale lantern from Galerie Van der Straeten, table by Robert Kuo 105tl White Flax pendant light by Jeremy Cole 105tr Swarovski crystal light 105mr Lézard Électrique wall light by Mathieu Lustrerie 105br Fluid pendant lights by Beau McClellan, table by Dellavista, chairs by Holly Hunt, benches from St Paul Home, carver chairs by Munna 107 bar designed by Kelly Hoppen Interiors, stools by India Mahdavi 109 chairs custom-made by Talisman 111r pendant light by OCHRE 112t mirror from David Gill Gallery 112b mirror by Christopher Guy, Aloe Blossom pendant light by Jeremy Cole, wall light Cinabre, coffee table by Kelly Hoppen, side table Promemoria 114 white ceramic Aloe Shoot pendant lights by Jeremy Cole, linen bench by Porta Romana 115tl mirror by DK Home 115bl reinterpretation of iconic Ball chair by Eero Aarnio 119l wall light by Stéphane Parmentier 121r resin coral branches from kellyhoppen.com 122 glass domes with resin coral from kellyhoppen.com 126l

console tables by Christian Liaigre 127 stools by India Mahdavi, pendant lights from Edition Limitée 130 pivoting shutters designed by Kelly Hoppen, bespoke table designed by Kelly Hoppen with bronze base by Matt Stanwix, pendant lights by Hervé Langlais for Galerie Negropontes, chairs from Gallerie 16 133 sofa by Andrée Putman (for Ralph Pucci), Swarovski crystal light, table by Robert Kuo 134l Velin banquettes by Christian Liaigre, lighting by Robert Clift 138 table from St Paul Home, Altar pendant light by Kevin Reilly, Saturn acrylic chairs by Andrew Martin, mirrors by DK Home, Hive pendant lights by Cravt Original 139 stools by India Mahdavi 140t Plaza armchair in white leather and Savoy lounge table by Modénature, Kolom pendant light by Kevin Reilly, silver tumblers by C Best 140b table by Modénature, pendant by Kevin Reilly 141t Wishbone chairs by Hans Wegner 141b Series 7 chairs by Arne Jacobsen 142 table and white leather chairs by Modénature, chainmail pendant light custommade by OCHRE 144 bespoke pendant light designed by Kelly Hoppen, Velin chairs, banquettes and Ajoure side table by Christian Liaigre, benches by Guillaume Alan, stools by Tom Dixon, glass bubble pendant lights designed by Kelly Hoppen with glass blown by DARK, armchairs by Kelly Hoppen, Sera Lantern floor lamp by Mark Brazier-Jones, pivoting lacquered doors designed by Kelly Hoppen, sofa from the Kelly Hoppen Collection 147t pendant light designed by Kelly Hoppen 147b Velin chairs and banquettes by Christian Liaigre, benches by Guillaume Alan, linear pendant light by Kelly Hoppen, Sera Lantern floor lamp (left) by Mark Brazier-Jones, Ribot lamp by DeCastelli (right) 148 bespoke pendant light designed by Kelly Hoppen, Velin chairs, banquettes and Ajoure side table by Christian Liaigre, benches by Guillaume Alan, stools by Tom Dixon, glass bubble pendant lights designed by Kelly Hoppen with glass blown by DARK, armchairs by Kelly Hoppen, Sera Lantern floor lamp by Mark Brazier-Jones, pivoting lacquered doors designed by Kelly Hoppen, sofa from the Kelly Hoppen Collection 149 bubble pendant lights by Kelly Hoppen with glass blown by DARK, bespoke linear pendant light designed by Kelly Hoppen, stools by Tom Dixon, Velin banquettes and chairs by Christian Liaigre, benches by Guillaume Alan 150 Gem Collection pendant lights by Tom Dixon, custom-made Munich table by Baltus, Diaz Due Chair by Meridiani, Dome Light by Aanngenaam XL, Large Swing Sconce by Jason Koharik, Newman sofa by Meridiani, Torre tables by Azadeh Shladovsky, vases by Anna Torfs 151 kitchen by Poggenpohl, Avico pendant light by Fontana Arte, ceramic vessels by Absolute Flowers 152 kitchen by Boffi 153

lighting by Robert Clift 157 pendant light (foreground) by Kelly Hoppen with glass bubbles blown by DARK, pendant light (background) Hervé Langlais for Galerie Negropontes, Globe table lamp by Lee Broom, sofa and armchairs from the Kelly Hoppen Collection, Ribot floor lamp DeCastelli, Sera Lantern floor lamp Mark Brazier-Jones 161 Torre stools by Azadeh Shladovsky 162 Galion console table by Christian Liaigre, metal-base floor lamps, round table with fluted base and nest of side tables by Robert Kuo, bowls by Anna Torfs 164l Metropolis fire sculpture by BD Design 165c coffee tables by Casamilano, pendants and floor lamp by Holly Hunt 166r chandeliers in gimbals by Arteinmotion, coffee tables by Oly Studio, armchairs by Kelly Hoppen, side tables by Sé, fireplace sculpture by BD Design, vases by Kelly Hoppen Ltd 167 White Flax pendant light by Jeremy Cole, Darder Wingback chairs by Holly Hunt, floor lamps by Robert Kuo, sofas by Rose Uniacke, coffee table by Kelly Hoppen, Rock side table by Hudson, metal side table Christian Liaigre, custom-made circular table by Robert Kuo 173b bedside lamps by OCHRE, pendant light by Tom Dixon, bed by Duxiana 174 Mirror Ball pendant light by Tom Dixon, Barcelona stool by Mies van der Rohe, bedside table from kellyhoppen.com, bed by Kelly Hoppen 178 glass pendant lights by OCHRE, damask bench and table lamp by Christian Liaigre, dressing table and stool by Spencer Fung, mirror by Rue de Lilles Paris, side tables from Sé 179b Inhale pendant light by Lasvit Lighting, Square Panel 02-060 wallpaper by Kelly Hoppen for Graham & Brown 184t bedside lamps by OCHRE, pendant light by Tom Dixon, bed by Duxiana 187 Harmony bathtub by Kelly Hoppen for Apaiser 190l Starlet bath by Bette, KH2 taps by Kelly Hoppen for Waterfront 191l cut-crystal and brass pendants by Lee Broom 192l ceramic sinks by Rifra 193l Origami basin and bath by Kelly Hoppen for Apaiser, side table from Sé 195 Harmony bath by Kelly Hoppen for Apaiser, Patera light sculpture by Niamh Barry

Publishing Credits:

Writer and Editor: Zia Mattocks
Designer: Clare Baggaley

Front cover photographed by Malcolm Menzies. Floor designed by Kelly Hoppen for Hakwood

Brimming with creative inspiration, how-to projects and useful information to enrich your everyday life, Quarto Knows is a favourite destination for those pursuing their interests and passions. Visit our site and dig deeper with our books into your area of interest: Quarto Creates, Quarto Cooks, Quarto Homes, Quarto Lives, Quarto Drives, Quarto Explores, Quarto Gifts, or Quarto Kids.

First published in 2021 by Frances Lincoln Publishing, an imprint of The Quarto Group.
The Old Brewery,
6 Blundell Street
London, N7 9BH,
United Kingdom
T (0)20 7700 6700
www.QuartoKnows.com

A catalogue record for this book is available from the British Library.

ISBN 978-0711262300

Ebook ISBN 978 0 7112 6231 7

10 9 8 7 6 5 4 3 2

Printed in Bosnia and Herzegovina

FSC
www.fsc.org
MIX
Paper from
responsible sources
FSC® C118234